AUGUSTINE'S CONFESSIONS AND SHAKESPEARE'S KING LEAR

READING AUGUSTINE

Series Editor:
Miles Hollingworth
In collaboration with the Wessel-Hollingworth Foundation

Reading Augustine presents books that offer personal, nuanced and oftentimes literary readings of Saint Augustine of Hippo. Each time, the idea is to treat Augustine as a spiritual and intellectual icon of the Western tradition, and to read through him to some or other pressing concern of our current day, or to some enduring issue or theme. In this way, the writers follow the model of Augustine himself, who produced his famous output of words and ideas in active tussle with the world in which he lived. When the series launched, this approach could raise eyebrows, but now that technology and pandemics have brought us into the world and society like never before, and when scholarship is expected to live the same way and responsibly, the series is well-set and thriving.

Volumes in the series include:
On Order, Authority, and Modern Civil-Military Relations, Lindsay P. Cohn
On Interrogation, Introspection, Dialectic and the Ineluctable Polarity of Being and Knowing, Matthew W. Knotts
On the Nature, Limits, Meaning, and End of Work, Zachary Thomas Settle
On Hellenism, Judaism, Individualism, and Early Christian Theories of the Subject, Guillermo M. Jodra
On Regular Life, Freedom, Modernity, and Augustinian Communitarianism, Guillermo M. Jodra
On The Confessions as 'confessio', Barry A. David
On Christology, Anthropology, Cognitive Science and the Human Body, Martin Claes
On Signs, Christ, Truth and the Interpretation of Scripture, Susannah Ticciati
On Images, Visual Culture, Memory and the Play without a Script, Matthias Smalbrugge
On Distance, Belonging, Isolation and the Quarantined Church of Today, Pablo Irizar
On Mystery, Ineffability, Silence, and Musical Symbolism, Laurence Wuidar
On King Lear, The Confessions, and Human Experience and Nature, Kim Paffenroth

AUGUSTINE'S CONFESSIONS AND SHAKESPEARE'S KING LEAR

POWER, PARENTHOOD, AND PRESENCE

Kim Paffenroth

BLOOMSBURY ACADEMIC
LONDON • NEW YORK • OXFORD • NEW DELHI • SYDNEY

BLOOMSBURY ACADEMIC

Bloomsbury Publishing Plc, 50 Bedford Square, London, WC1B 3DP, UK
Bloomsbury Publishing Inc, 1359 Broadway, New York, NY 10018, USA
Bloomsbury Publishing Ireland, 29 Earlsfort Terrace, Dublin 2, D02 AY28, Ireland

BLOOMSBURY, BLOOMSBURY ACADEMIC and the Diana logo are trademarks of Bloomsbury Publishing Plc

First published in Great Britain 2026

Copyright © Kim Paffenroth, 2026

Kim Paffenroth has asserted his right under the Copyright, Designs and Patents Act, 1988, to be identified as Author of this work.

For legal purposes the Acknowledgments on pp. vi–vii constitute an extension of this copyright page.

Cover design: Lara Himpelmann
Cover Illustration by Monika Jurczyk / Adobe Stock

All rights reserved. No part of this publication may be: i) reproduced or transmitted in any form, electronic or mechanical, including photocopying, recording or by means of any information storage or retrieval system without prior permission in writing from the publishers; or ii) used or reproduced in any way for the training, development or operation of artificial intelligence (AI) technologies, including generative AI technologies. The rights holders expressly reserve this publication from the text and data mining exception as per Article 4(3) of the Digital Single Market Directive (EU) 2019/790.

Bloomsbury Publishing Plc does not have any control over, or responsibility for, any third-party websites referred to or in this book. All internet addresses given in this book were correct at the time of going to press. The author and publisher regret any inconvenience caused if addresses have changed or sites have ceased to exist, but can accept no responsibility for any such changes.

A catalogue record for this book is available from the British Library.

ISBN: HB: 978-1-3505-0088-4
PB: 978-1-3505-0087-7
ePDF: 978-1-3505-0090-7
eBook: 978-1-3505-0089-1

Series: Reading Augustine

Typeset by Newgen Knowledge Works Pvt. Ltd., Chennai, India
Printed and bound in Great Britain

For product safety related questions contact productsafety@bloomsbury.com.

To find out more about our authors and books visit www.bloomsbury.com and sign up for our newsletters.

CONTENTS

Acknowledgments vi

Introduction: Origins and Ends 1

1 **Augustine and Power** 7

2 **Lear and Power** 29

3 **Augustine and Women in** *Confessions* 55

4 **Women in** *King Lear* 75

5 **Conclusion** 91

Epilogue 105

Bibliography 115
Index 121

ACKNOWLEDGMENTS

As before, my editor, Miles Hollingworth (whom I still haven't met in person!) deserves the most credit for making this book happen. He has given me encouragement throughout to persevere and usefully expand my ideas, presenting them in a hopefully intelligible and convincing form. Everything in these pages would have remained inchoate thoughts, personal musings, and disconnected observations without him.

Team teaching was discontinued recently where I work, but the classes I previously taught there with Drs. Scott Cleary and Amy Stackhouse gave me much of the material included here, and they remain friends and supporters. Going further back in time and farther away geographically, Michael Gathje (formerly of Borders in Bryn Mawr, PA); Robert Kennedy of St. Francis Xavier University, Nova Scotia, who was a friend when I attended the University of Notre Dame; Bill Lebeda, with whom I attended Los Alamos High School; Sherry Truffin of Campbell University; and John Verdi, who was my advisor when I was an undergrad at St. John's College, Annapolis, have been frequent correspondents and critics as I wrote. To paraphrase Augustine, the unfeigned affection of true friends makes the difficulties of this life bearable, and sometimes even enables one to thrive and not just survive.

I am again happy to thank the staff at Iona University's Ryan Library, under the direction of Richard Palladino (now emeritus), along with the Assistant Director of Libraries, Natalka C. Sawchuk, and the Serials and Electronic Resources Librarian, Casey Hampsey. I note especially Ed Helmrich and his staff in the Interlibrary Loan office for their help in obtaining books and articles from other libraries. Finally, I would add the deepest appreciation for Dr. Charlotte Wray, my assistant when I was directing the Honors Program at Iona University (when I began this writing project). She was always a huge help to students and to me, whatever little errand or assistance any of us needed. She made my time as Director successful and never got the recognition she should have.

And if friends make difficulties bearable, and persistent editors make writing possible, and university staff make research easier, I think I will

Acknowledgments

always find the potential and future orientation of young people to be a special source of energy and joy: for me, they are the most reliable source of hope. And I think this has become clearer in late middle age and has been focused on both by my vocation as an educator and my identity as a parent. Among recent graduates, I have been variously inspired by Alyssa Lewandowski, Wanda McDonald, and Emily Varker. Continuing or resuming my friendships with Madeleine Bennett, Alysha Gagnon, Angela Harris, and Danny Perrier, who were in my classes many years ago, were also sources of inspiration—as were resuming conversations with them about texts we had studied together. The curiosity and enthusiasm of all these young people in class, and their elegant writing, have helped me better form and express my thoughts here, and throughout the time I've known them. And seeing the accomplishments in journalism and art wrought by my adult, biological children, Charles and Sophia, and their growth in life and relationships, is a constant source of pride and wonder to me, especially when I consider that I began my writing career marveling at their birth and infancy—at their simply existing and living—and now they're like real human beings who do stuff.

INTRODUCTION
ORIGINS AND ENDS

To begin a sequel to an earlier work presents the challenge of simultaneously starting something new, while also showing how something that previously seemed finished is, from a new perspective, incomplete, and now needs more to show its full meaning. It is to begin something that could not exist without its predecessor, but which thereby changes what had been a single book into a preface or first volume. It is both a continuation and an alteration, so in a way, it is a very presumptuous step to take. But by doing so, it also makes a statement about the author, that his/her outlook and view have changed or grown and now require further explanation to make sense or be true anymore. It is therefore an acknowledgment of our changeable and incomplete nature as we struggle to tell a fuller but still (perhaps always) incomplete story. So from a different point of view, it is a humbler undertaking than authorship often is, with its implication that, "Here is my story," or even, "Here is *the* story," you need to read, because a sequel admits by its very existence that, "Here is how I needed to change my story since the last time I tried (with only partial success) to put it into words." In this, perhaps, as different as the method and content are today, I return again to versions of the questions I began considering thirty years ago, when my first professional writings were on the synoptic gospels and how they altered and adapted traditions that came to them, changing the Gospel of Mark into the Gospel of Luke and then adding the Book of Acts.

In the previous (now first) volume, I presented a series of "problems" around which both Augustine's *Confessions* and Shakespeare's *King Lear* revolve, or to which they return in their various ways—love, language, nature, and reason.[1] The strength (if I may) of this method was that two texts of different genres, from different authors and eras, could illuminate both their points of similarity and highlight their differences, giving both complementarity, completion, and contrast. But in reflecting on this

---

[1] Kim Paffenroth, *On King Lear, the Confessions, and Human Experience and Nature*. Reading Augustine Series (New York: Bloomsbury, 2021).

arrangement, I also saw what my analysis was lacking and where I wanted to go with it now. I saw clearly, in hindsight, what was limited in my perspective and what needed to be added. Post-pandemic, nearing old as opposed to middle aged, and with new and unexpected challenges in my life, the texts and what I wanted to say based on them had changed—probably more than in any other period of similar length in my life. Reflecting on Augustine's life, and on various readings, performances, and analyses of *King Lear*, two subjects only cursorily and peripherally touched on in my earlier volume called for more attention and drew me to elaborate their significance and meaning—God, and the women in the male protagonists' lives.

Indeed, as I have thought about this current volume, I might give a balanced and opposite view of the two texts I'm examining: Augustine in *Confessions* claims his life and story revolve around God, but it is really women who center and guide him; and *King Lear* more obviously revolves around women characters (antagonists), while leaving God out of the story, but constantly coming very close to something like belief (or at least hope) in Him. So it is not just a matter of filling in something I had omitted before, but finally reckoning with what makes these two texts work for or on us. Focusing on certain aspects of God and women would bring the current work's title more into line with others in the *Reading Augustine* series (which mostly have the form of "Augustine and Three Abstract Nouns, and alliteration is a bonus"). It would also allow me to respond to and incorporate into my analysis the comments of reviewers and others on the first volume.[2]

Those reviews have made me more sensitive to the differences between the two texts I'm examining. I think I have a tendency, in my eagerness to draw connections, to brush aside or minimize differences whose honest and thorough evaluation is more helpful than noticing and elaborating a surface similarity. Or worse, I become so committed to an elaborate analysis that I insist on similarities rather than acknowledging differences. This caution was especially helpful in the chapters on "power," because as much as I still insist these two texts are vitally and revealingly similar in how they depict a virtuous and meaningful life, the similarity I finally assert can only be appreciated and understood if their differences on God's existence are fully acknowledged. I am deeply grateful to the reviewers for improving

---

[2] So far, I have read the following reviews: Hannibal Hamlin, "Review of Kim Paffenroth: *On King Lear, the Confessions, and Human Experience and Nature*." *Augustinian Studies* 54.1 (2023): 117–21; Esther Lisa Freinkel Tishman, "Review of Kim Paffenroth: *On King Lear, the Confessions, and Human Experience and Nature*." *Augustiniana* 72.3–4 (2022): 427–30.

Introduction: Origins and Ends

the current analysis in this way. I am also appreciative of and gratified by how they highlighted for me the biases I have that I am not so eager to get beyond. The reviews I have read noted the (at times severe, to them) limitations of my close reading, but also praised it as a heuristic to certain tendencies of modernity in general and current US politics in particular—that my analysis took them away from a "doomscrolling, media-saturated, MAGA-afflicted, post?-pandemic world,"[3] and from "Trump's alternative facts and the outright delusions of QAnon."[4] I could never have guessed I would be the anti-Trump of Augustine scholars (or of anything, really). But clearly, with a second Trump term upon us now, I will have to adjust and perhaps embrace my new phase of truth-telling. Both reviews ended with a feeling that my analysis had returned them to an earlier, simpler time, the memory of which is pleasant, healthful, and invigorating to our current situation: "He [Paffenroth] tells me something I already knew, but it was something I needed to remember about good literature and the balm to be found there";[5] "Paffenroth's readings are acute and often refreshing for an honesty and openness too rare in literary criticism."[6] If the current work reminds you why you enjoyed and found spiritual and intellectual succor in *King Lear* and *Confessions* at some point long ago (or more recently) and makes you want to go back for more (or pick up a new text with hopeful promises of such)—that, to me, is a more valuable accomplishment, a deeper devotion to the truth, than being correct on some small and difficult point of interpretation.

Continuing with this analysis that is naïve but in some way perhaps convincing (or at least endearing) in its candor and nostalgia, it continued to make me wonder, as I wondered in the introduction to the previous volume, why I noticed these things only now, after reading, studying, and writing on these texts for decades. After all, it is somewhat embarrassing, as a supposed or reputed theologian or religious scholar, to write (again) a book that deals almost exclusively with people (yes, mostly men—though that particular limitation has seldom embarrassed my predecessors in most religious traditions) and barely mentions God. And I probably cannot fully answer this, because I now see more clearly that my point is that the drive to find answers, to solve "problems," as I framed it in the first volume, is

---

[3] Tishman, "Review," 427.
[4] Hamlin, "Review," 117.
[5] Tishman, "Review," 430.
[6] Hamlin, "Review," 120.

as limiting as it is revealing: it shapes the discourse, determines what is included and what is ignored, more fundamentally than the kinds of questions asked. And such propositional thinking does not lend itself to talking about God (as opposed to dissecting and analyzing one's innermost thoughts, like Augustine, or articulating them on stage, as Lear does), or to trying to imagine what effect other people have on one (as opposed to what one does or intends to do oneself). To talk about how one loves (or hates) one's God, or one's mother, or one's partner; or how those beings love oneself; or the part one's God, mother, or partner has played in one's life and formation; or how one has affected them—these are not best expressed by propositions or facts about the human or divine object, but by speculation and imagination. It may not be quite ineffable, but it is more a matter of experiences than propositions, as is witnessing a performance of the play, or even reading scenes as not strictly logical (though chosen and written by someone as logical as Augustine) but as confounding and uncanny as Augustine's descriptions of his overwhelming grief at the deaths of his friend (Book 4) and mother (Book 9), or of his sudden and dreaded but longed for "conversion" (Book 8).

Moreover, to continue with blunt candor: my inclination will always be that talking directly and explicitly about God is less helpful, less revelatory (ironically), than talking about a myriad of things related indirectly to Him. (Which I suppose would finally be everything, potentially.) We Americans now have mandated that the Ten Commandments be displayed in every classroom, as a kind of absurdly blatant advertisement of piety or orthodoxy, but usually deem it too difficult or divisive (or just rude), to talk seriously and openly about the spiritual dimensions or religious significance of our relationships or the art and literature we consume, cordoning those off for only objective, neutral analysis (if we bother to analyze them at all).

The differences between the two texts examined here lead to a difference in how the sections are presented here. In the first volume, we had four "problems," each of which had a chapter analyzing it in both *Confessions* and *King Lear*. Here the section on God has two chapters on the broader concept of power in general (the protagonists' own, and their acceptance or confrontation with that of others, including the supposedly infinitely powerful Being, God)—one on Augustine (Chapter 1) and one on *King Lear* (Chapter 2). The protagonists' relationships with women are the topics of the next two chapters—on *Confessions* (Chapter 3) and on *King Lear* (Chapter 4). A concluding chapter considers how both protagonists, in their different ways and with varying degrees of success or permanence, find ways to be fully, honestly, and authentically present to themselves and others. An epilogue returns to some of the issues raised here in the introduction, as to where and how in my own life these questions formed and how they may play out now.

In offering less in the way of "answers" to "problems," and more of exploration or examination, I hope I am better acknowledging the inadequacy and distortion of asserting (intellectual or mental) power over a person or idea: indeed, such is just a rarefied or intellectualized or sublimated version of physical domination, and just as doomed to fail and injure. I have tried to approach writing this time, not so much like a puzzle to be solved, but more like a well-worn instrument to play with and enjoy again, in ways that are both familiar and novel.

CHAPTER 1
AUGUSTINE AND POWER

Power is the quality with which the (mostly) fictitious Lear and the real but embellished and selectively remembered Augustine most resemble one another. Both Lear and Augustine are—to begin by being blunt and somewhat dismissive—typical white male protagonists. (Yes, debatable as to the amount of melanin in the case of Augustine, but certainly imagined as white and European by many who have since called him "saint.") They do heroic stuff; they overcome obstacles through their own efforts. And their qualities of being white and male are not "typical" in a good sense— not an advantage or normative—from our perspective. And they are not "typical" in a statistical sense—most people in the past or now are not male and white. But they are the norm in the Western canon, of whatever genre we consider (political, philosophical, literary, musical, and artistic). So, they are typical in a sense that would make many readers or critics today rather skeptical of their value to us now: just another couple of dead, white men who wrote a book and/or had a book written about them (both, in Augustine's case).

But like most of the characters of world literature before the nineteenth century, Lear and Augustine cannot (I don't think) themselves question or problematize their gender or race because they are blissfully unaware of it, at least in their own case. Race was so much a non-issue for Augustine that we are left wondering and speculating how dark-skinned he really was. Shakespeare shows more awareness of race, but not in this play set in pre-Christian England. (And anyone who experiences contemporary productions of the play has seen casts of all different races, which does not raise any comment, because it is never noted in the dialogue: the characters are unaware of their race, and the actors are pretending to be so.) Gender is more complicated: Lear questions his own masculinity (but not his maleness), and both Lear and Augustine have difficult interactions with females (indeed, interactions made more difficult by their antagonists' attitude toward gender). But that is why the protagonists' relationships with women will occupy us in later chapters.

So it does come back to questions related to the exercise of power—to their "doing stuff," or being able to tolerate others doing stuff to them. I don't think Lear or Augustine would quite understand the meaning if they were accused of "toxic masculinity" (as I and many others have had occasion to label them), but both of them do painfully come to realize the "toxic" part of their behavior—they just would have called it selfishness, sinfulness, cruelty, or abuse of power (without gendering it). And this does show a way in which they are less typical in world literature: their doing stuff is not primarily about military exploits or political rule—like, for example, Odysseus or Beowulf—but about personal growth or change or development, overcoming obstacles within themselves. Both our subjects are old, powerful, white men, learning about the limits and responsibilities of their power: Lear, the king of all the Britons when the play opens and fully empowered to make everyone else on stage very satisfied or miserable; Augustine, by the time of his writing *Confessions*, a bishop leading the church, deciding its doctrines and policies as it grew throughout the first part of his life, to the point that it defeated all rival sects and outlived the empire itself, by the end of his life. Unlike the other qualities we will consider, where the trajectories of their lives are quite different (on the existence of God and in their relationships with women), on being very powerful men, they are very similar when we first meet them. And they both analyze and problematize their relationship with power because both reflect on it and how its right exercise could fulfill them and its incorrect use could degrade them.

To focus now on Augustine: we will throughout have to remind ourselves of the differences between Augustine the character in *Confessions* and Augustine the author narrating and theorizing on those events many years later. By the time he wrote *Confessions*, he was a bishop, and indeed the book was meant to inform his readers and followers and colleagues what kind of man, cleric, leader, and believer he was.[1] So, the deep significances ascribed to events must be carefully sifted and considered by us, to distinguish between those ideas that could plausibly have occurred to Augustine the character

---

[1] See Peter Brown, *Augustine of Hippo: A Biography*. Forty-Fifth Anniversary Edition (Berkeley and Los Angeles: University of California Press, 2000; first published 1967) 154–55: "Augustine wrote his Confessions at some time around 397, that is, only a few years after he had become a bishop in Africa… he will tell his readers exactly how he still had to struggle with his own temptations."

when these events happened to him as a younger man, and those, on the other hand, that are the fully elaborated analyses of a middle-aged cleric. But at the same time, we should be alert to even the young Augustine's sensitivity and acuity—as well as to the old Augustine's awareness of his own ambiguity or inconsistency: it is not as though Augustine the character simply stumbled about as a thoughtless, careless youth, unaware of the implications or associations of his thoughts and actions, and the author Augustine came along and imposed or projected (or fabricated) order and orthodoxy on the previously unexamined chaos of his former life. It is more like the multifaceted and multivalent human experience that was immediate, vivid, and confusing to the young Augustine could be described and analyzed with more detail and context by the older, authorial Augustine, perhaps losing some of its confusion or frustration but retaining its sense of awe and complexity and adding previously unrealized order and connections. This book retains its power and persuasiveness precisely because there is no simplistic tidiness and consistency here, either from youthful ignorance or mature dogma.[2]

The opening paragraph of *Confessions* is, appropriately, a clear and forceful summary of Augustine's full, mature thought on what the events of his life mean:

> Great are you, O Lord, and exceedingly worth of praise; your power is immense, and your wisdom beyond reckoning. And so we humans, who are a due part of your creation, long to praise you – we who carry our mortality about with us,[3] carry the evidence of our sin and with it the proof that you thwart the proud. Yet these humans, due part of your creation as they are, still do long to praise you. You stir us so that

---

[2] Cf. Brown, *Augustine of Hippo*, 156:

> No matter how much Augustine wished to share the ideals of a group, he remained irreducibly eccentric. He had still a lot to explain about himself... Augustine the *servus Dei*, Augustine the bishop, had remained very much Augustine; and his *Confessions* could not have communicated this to his friends with greater charm, persuasiveness, and with a determination all the more unanswerable for being addressed not to a human audience, but to God.

[3] Acknowledgment of our mortality is something Lear realizes over the course of the play, as at *King Lear* 4.6.147148: "GLOUCESTER: O, let me kiss that hand! LEAR Let me wipe it first; it smells of mortality." As on many points, the author Augustine fully realizes this and announces it here at the beginning of the text, but the character Augustine, like Lear, is only coming to understand it in the events he's writing down and analyzing years later.

praising you may bring us joy, because you have made us and drawn us to yourself, and our heart is unquiet until it rests in you.[4]

Everything in human life is a conflict between a right, originally directed orientation toward God, and a sinful misdirection away from God.

So although he begins by acknowledging, praising, and thanking God for the right orientation that still exists in all humans, himself included, he believes now, in his mature analysis, that most of our lives and actions are sinful and take us further away from God. So many things that to us seem "normal" or neutral or even positive behavior, Augustine proclaims are, in fact, sinful. And to make his point as vividly as possible, Augustine starts out with some of his more shocking examples—that babies crying are indeed, from his adult perspective and analysis, sinful. But how? Clearly not from any sense of deliberation or consciousness: Augustine is fully aware the infant is not deliberately or knowingly doing anything—they are just flailing about and making inarticulate noises—so how can it be sinful? Is it just the overwhelming, unavoidable desire of hunger bursting forth in incoherent, uncontrollable screams from an infant? That would surely be our first description if we've seen and heard a hungry baby. If desire itself is sinful, then yes, everyone is sinful, but at some animal level for which we could not repent or be healed, anymore than we could repent of perspiring when it's hot outside, or for our hair and nails growing without our knowledge or consent.[5] And Augustine seems veering close to theorizing a depth of sinfulness as ingrained and fundamental to us as this would imply. But he stops short, insisting that all such urges for preservation, existence, even thriving, are God-given and therefore good and praiseworthy:

> Your will is that I should praise you, O Lord my God, who gave life and a body to that infant; you will me to praise you who equipped him with faculties, built up his limbs, and adorned him with a distinctive shape, as we can see. You implanted in him all the urges proper to a living creature

---

[4]*Conf.* 1.1.1, *The Confessions* (trans. Maria Boulding; ed. John E. Rotelle; Hyde Park, NY: New City Press, 1997). Used with permission. All quotations from *Confessions* are from this translation unless otherwise noted.

[5]The Manichaean *reductio ad absurdum* mentioned by Augustine in *Conf.* 3.7.12 that "disproves" God could ever have a body, lest He have the limitations of hair and nails: "I was being subtly maneuvered into accepting the views of those stupid deceivers by the questions they constantly asked me about the origin of evil, and whether God was confined to a material form with hair and nails."

Augustine and Power

to ensure his coherence and safety; and now you command me to praise you for those gifts, and to confess to you and sing to your name, O Most High, because you are God, almighty and good, and would be so even if you had wrought no other works than these, since none but yourself, the only God, can bring them into existence. From you derives all manner of being, O God most beautiful, who endow all things with their beautiful form and by your governance direct them in their due order.[6]

Therefore, there has to be one more detail to his supposed observations of infants—their behavior toward others trying to share in this feast, and what Augustine surmises about their attitudes, by observing their outward behavior:

> The only innocent feature in babies is the weakness of their frames; the minds of infants are far from innocent. I have watched and experienced for myself the jealousy of a small child: he could not even speak, yet he glared with livid fury at his fellow-nursling. Everyone has seen this. Mothers and nurses claim to have some means of their own to charm away such behavior. Is this to be regarded as innocence, this refusal to tolerate a rival for a richly abundant fountain of milk, at a time when the other child stands in greatest need of it and depends for its very life on this food alone? Behavior of this kind is cheerfully condoned, however, not because it is trivial or of small account, but because everyone knows that it will fade away as the baby grows up. This is clear from the fact that those same actions are by no means calmly tolerated if detected in anyone of more mature years.[7]

It is not just hunger, or even the reflexive vocalization coming from hunger, as annoying as those are to the adults around the babies, but "jealousy" and "fury" coming from the infant mind (even if its limbs are too weak or incapable to act on such urges)—feelings that are not conducive to its safety and well-being (and therefore not from God, and therefore not praiseworthy but blameworthy).[8] It is the urge, not to feed, but to stop another from

---

[6]*Conf.* 1.7.12.
[7]*Conf.* 1.7.11.
[8]Just above, *Conf.* 1.6.8, Augustine notes such outbursts may be physically harmful to the infant (not just sinful). And cf. Marianne Novy, *Love's Argument: Gender Relations in Shakespeare* (Chapel Hill and London: University of North Carolina Press, 1984) 152, on the similarity

feeding—to dominate, oppress, exert power over another for no good it will do oneself, but just because domination itself is a sinful urge we have from birth, and power is, to our sinful mind, a good in itself we feel we must pursue.[9]

Thus, Book 1 begins with a striking example of what we discussed above—the difference between the perspective of the character Augustine and that of the author Augustine, since the infant (character) thinks nothing of what's happening, but the author has an elaborate (and shocking) analysis of it. Further, it is striking for how far Augustine will bend or stretch an example to fit his analysis: as noted, our first, commonsensical analysis of a crying baby would be to label it as hungry or overcome by desire; but Augustine knows that may be the most annoying part of a baby's behavior to everyone else, but it cannot be the basis or cause of sin. (Sins of excessive appetite, called by Aristotle and Christian moralists following his analysis, "sins of incontinence," are only sins if the person can restrain and direct them, and refrains from doing so, and that is clearly not the case for infants.) For that, he has to bring in the *libido dominandi*, the urge to dominate, as fanciful as such an analysis may be in the case of supposedly glaring infants, who he thinks are capable of feelings as primitive, but still complex as "jealousy."

Similar analyses continue in Book 1. Growth as momentous and potentially humane as the acquisition of speech he notes, but quickly moves from communication and fellowship to the further opportunities it offers for conflict among humans:

> In this way I gradually built up a collection of words, observing them as they were used in their proper places in different sentences and hearing them frequently. I came to understand which things they signified, and by schooling my own mouth to utter them I declared my wishes by using the same signs. Thus I learned to express my needs to the people among whom I lived, and they made their wishes known to me; and I waded deeper into the stormy world of human life, although

---

between infants and kings, on this point of their tyrannical behavior: "but it has been less observed that the similarity between king and child is in part in their assumptions of omnipotence encouraged – for different reasons – by the flattery of those who care for them."
[9]It is also driven by fear of loss, rather than desire for acquisition, Augustine realizes. Cf. Joseph J. McInerney, foreword by Chad C. Pecknold, *The Greatness of Humility: St. Augustine on Moral Excellence* (Cambridge, England: James Clarke, 2017) 58: "Since often times the impediments to material goods are other people, lovers of these goods resort to evil and crime against others in order to safeguard or acquire possession of those goods."

I was still subject to the authority of my parents and the guidance of my elders.[10]

When the protagonist in *Dead Poets Society* (1989) first encounters his youthful charges, he asks them what language is for. One of them naively, and by rote, intones, "To express thoughts and ideas." The romantic protagonist shouts, "No! To woo women!" To appreciate (and be appropriately aghast at) Augustine's point, we should imagine him answering the same question with the grim and terrifying answer, "No. To deceive. To mislead. To exploit. To harm."

Moving on in Book 1, with his interactions with people multiplying and expanding (but not necessarily improving), what does Augustine remember of school days? Play? Learning? Achievements? Praise? Not really—or at least it is not what he chooses to recount later and is subject to scrutiny and analysis. Rather, he dwells on and details violence from adults (more domination, and not the impotent infant kind, but with physical power to inflict lasting, memorable harm, and fully sanctioned by custom and law); and laziness, jealousy, and disobedience from children. And all of it only to gain reputation and money (more sins, and of a decidedly more adult kind). When he nods toward some positive outcome of education, it is only what God brings about, despite the sinfulness of teachers, learners, and often even the subject matter itself:

> Yet even during that time of my boyhood, when it was supposed that I was safer than I would be in adolescence, I was not fond of study, and hated being driven to it. Driven I was, though, and that did me good, though my own attitude was far from good, because I learned only under compulsion, and no one is doing right who acts unwillingly, even if what he does is good in itself. The people who forced me on were not acting well either, but good accrued to me all the same from you, My God. They did not foresee to what use I would put the lessons they made me learn: they thought only of sating man's insatiable appetite for a poverty tricked out as wealth and a fame that is but infamy. But you, who have even kept count of our hairs, turned to my profit the misguided views of those who stood over me and made me learn, just as you also turned to my profit my own perverse unwillingness to

---

[10]*Conf.* 1.8.13.

> learn by using it to punish me, for I certainly deserved punishment, being a great sinner for such a tiny boy. In this way you turned to my good the actions of those who were doing no good, and gave me my just desserts by means of my sin itself. Matters are so arranged at your command that every disordered soul is its own punishment.[11]

As dark as Augustine's vision of human nature often seems, he reminds us (and we must remind ourselves that it is at the heart of his thinking and writing) that God turns everything, even (or especially) sin, to His own good, loving ends—but almost always in spite of human agents, not because of their cooperation.

Book 2 brings us to probably the most famous and memorable scene of *Confessions*, other than the "conversion" of Book 8—the young Augustine's theft of pears. More so than his analysis of glaring babies, his account here is a mixture of thoughts that may have occupied the sixteen-year-old mind of Augustine, blending now seamlessly (and at times confusingly) with ideas that can only be from a 45-year-old cleric and theologian composing the story. And similar to Augustine's bending of his analysis of infants to be more about power and domination than we might have expected, so here his analysis moves from thoughtless vandalism (certainly the most frequent and most complex bad behavior I was capable of at that age), to something more like blasphemous, creaturely, almost Miltonian rebellion (which I would hesitate to label anything I've ever done, no matter how conniving or dastardly or mature).

Augustine's account of the pear tree theft begins with a combination of youthful activity and thought, with much later reflection woven into the description:

> Close to our vineyard there was a pear tree laden with fruit. This fruit was not enticing, either in appearance or in flavor. We nasty lads went there to shake down the fruit and carry it off at dead of night, after prolonging our games out of doors until that late hour according to our abominable custom. We took enormous quantities, not to feast on ourselves but perhaps to throw to the pigs; we did eat a few, but that was not our motive: we derived pleasure from the deed simply because it was forbidden.[12]

---

[11] *Conf.* 1.12.19.
[12] *Conf.* 2.4.9.

Augustine and Power

The motivelessness of evil (which at its extreme would mean that pure evil cannot exist because existence itself is a good) is part of Augustine's mature analysis—and a difficult part for him to articulate throughout the early books of *Confessions*, under the more material conception of the Manichees (i.e., the understanding he held at the time these events actually occurred).[13] But it is implicit in the actions of teenage Augustine: he stole without wanting or keeping the things he stole. And he had just narrated, very offhandedly, more casual, habitual, "regular" thefts (*Conf.* 1.19.30) that did include using or consuming the stolen goods: this scene sticks out because it really was different, even at the time, in execution and motive. And as I observed above about my own youthful criminality, while blasphemy and idolatry might seem a bit much to describe anything I did at the time, I think I would have admitted to enjoying destruction for its own sake, as Augustine observed of himself:

> Look upon my heart, O God, look upon this heart of mine, on which you took pity in its abysmal depths. Enable my heart to tell you now what it was seeking in this action which made me bad for no reason, in which there was no motive for my malice except malice. The malice was loathsome, and I loved it. I was in love with my own ruin, in love with decay: not with the thing for which I was falling into decay but with decay itself, for I was depraved in soul, and I leapt down from your strong support into destruction, hungering not for some advantage to be gained by the foul deed, but for the foulness of it.[14]

This does not seem an incredible admission for a self-reflective teenager, if more eloquent than I would have been capable of at that age—if asked why I broke or set fire to something, I probably would just have said, "Because

---

[13] Cf. McInerney, *Greatness of Humility*, 59–60: "Pride even makes the otherwise unfathomable reasoning behind Augustine's adolescent theft of the pears comprehensible, if not reasonable.... It is the perverse desire to act with impunity and autonomy along with the companionship of his fellow thieves that drives him to the theft." On the implications of the Manichaean view, see Gerald W. Schlabach, "Augustine's Hermeneutic of Humility: An Alternative to Moral Imperialism and Moral Relativism," *The Journal of Religious Ethics* 22.2 (1994) 299–330, esp. 310: "To call the will a discrete faculty is virtually equivalent to calling it a (potentially evil) substance within us, and once we do that we have something else to blame, something that allows us to evade confessing."
[14] *Conf.* 2.4.9.

it's fun"; or perhaps more honestly, "Because I'm bored"; or perhaps most revealingly, "Because I can't think of anything better to do." Augustine just takes the stock phrase, "For the hell of it," and unpacks it more fully and literally than we would normally.

Augustine continues to analyze the scene by recalling and expanding on the fact that it was done in a crowd of friends:

> The beautiful form of material things attracts our eyes, so we are drawn to gold, silver and the like. We are powerfully influenced by the feel of things agreeable to the touch, and each of our other senses finds some quality that appeals to it individually in the variety of material objects. There is the same appeal in worldly rank, and the possibility it offers of commanding and dominating other people: this too holds its attraction, and often provides an opportunity for settling old scores. We may seek all these things, O Lord, but in seeking them we must not deviate from your law. The life we live here is open to temptation by reason of a certain measure and harmony between its own splendor and all these beautiful things of low degree. Again, the friendship which draws human beings together in a tender bond is sweet to us because out of many minds it forges a unity. Sin gains entrance through these and similar good things when we turn to them with immoderate desire, since they are the lowest kind of goods and we thereby turn away from the truth and your law. These lowest goods hold delights for us indeed, but no such delights as does my God, who made all things; for in him the just man finds delight, and for upright souls he himself is joy.[15]

The expanded analysis on all the various things that attract us away from the proper love of God (sensory pleasures, the allure of fame and rank), which includes friendship (his main point here), is surely from the author Augustine. But the core insight on which it is built ("the friendship which draws human beings together in a tender bond is sweet to us") is a statement that sounds entirely plausible from a sensitive youth: youth may be wasted on the young, and they may not appreciate the bonds they have at that age, but they are not so oblivious as to be unable to state simply and accurately, "It is pleasant to have friends."

---

[15] *Conf.* 2.5.10.

But the implications of that bare statement vex and confuse the middle-aged Augustine, and I think certainly could not have occurred to him at the time these events occurred. (Again, to compare it to my own development: I would have said at sixteen that I liked having friends, but it never would have occurred to me to say why, or what the friendship was for, beyond pleasant interactions.) It is seven long paragraphs of sometimes convoluted discussion before Augustine can get back to a simple statement of what he was feeling or thinking at the time:

> What fruit did I ever reap from those things which I now blush to remember, and especially from the theft in which I found nothing to love save the theft itself, wretch that I was? It was nothing, and by the very act of committing it I became more wretched still. And yet, as I recall my state of mind at the time, I would not have done it alone; I most certainly would not have done it alone. It follows, then, that I also loved the camaraderie with my fellow-thieves. So it is not true to say that I loved nothing other than the theft? Ah, but it is true, because that gang- mentality too was a nothing. What was it in fact? Who can teach me, except the one who illumines my heart and distinguishes between its shadows? Why has this question come into my mind now, to be examined and discussed and considered? If the object of my love had been the pears I stole, and I simply wanted to enjoy them, I could have done it alone; similarly, if the act of committing the sin had sufficed by itself to yield me the pleasure I sought, I would have further inflamed my itching desire by the stimulation of conspiracy. But since my pleasure did not lie in the pears, it must have been in the crime as committed in the company of others who shared in the sin.[16]

Though again, he adds later analysis, which he even notes as subsequent commentary and not a recollection of what he was thinking at the time ("Why has this question come into my mind now"). I think moderns would give something more like the quick and incomplete analysis that the teenage Augustine gives of his actions: "peer pressure" led him into bad choices. It is only the mature Augustine who unpacks further questions of what is the value or purpose of friendship, how does it rank relative to other goods in this life, etc.

---

[16]*Conf.* 2.8.16.

Augustine's Confessions and Shakespeare's King Lear

Within that long detour on the part played by peer pressure in the theft, Augustine comes to a conclusion even more surprising than his tyrannical babies analysis because he is now asking not "What do they want?" (when what the baby wants seems clear—food—and Augustine is trying to tease out some further, hidden and more frightening implication of what they really want, domination) but, "What did I want, when I didn't want *anything*?" or even more precisely, "What did I want, when I didn't want *any **thing***?" And peer pressure does not seem enough to him: it is a facilitation, a necessary precursor of the act, but he is still left wondering, years later, what did he want or love when he reached for the forbidden pears?

> With regard to my theft, then: what did I love in it, and in what sense did I imitate my Lord, even if only with vicious perversity? Did the pleasure I sought lie in breaking the law at least in that sneaky way, since I was unable to do so with any show of strength? Was I, in truth a prisoner, trying to simulate a crippled sort of freedom, attempting a shady parody of omnipotence by getting away with something forbidden? How like that servant of yours who fled from his Lord and hid in the shadows! What rottenness, what a misshapen life! Rather a hideous pit of death! To do what was wrong simply because it was wrong – could I have found pleasure in that?[17]

Here is an analysis that must have been formulated with difficulty, with much thought concentrated on the event—not the spontaneous reaction at the time. No teenager (and not many adults) has ever connected the dots, in looking back at some senseless, trivial act, and thought, "Oh, I see: I was trying to be God! I secretly long for omnipotence. Now I get it!" But to give Augustine's point the credit it deserves: the overwhelming urge to dominate and exert arbitrary power over another person is not confined (unfortunately) to tyrants, serial killers, and a handful of villainous and powerful people. It is manifested daily in the actions of abusive spouses, cruel bullies, tyrannical bosses: or, as Augustine tries to reveal honestly—all of us in many of our interactions. By carefully and surprisingly unearthing it in such seemingly annoying and trivial, but unrelated and easily contained behaviors as the habits of glaring babies and bored teenagers, Augustine is

---

[17] *Conf.* 2.6.14.

trying to show the ubiquity of the abuse of power, its seductive and pervasive hold on everyone (even or especially those who have no real power).

Book 3 is mostly concerned with issues of belief, with Augustine's first encounter with philosophy in Cicero's *Hortensius*, his failed attempts to read the Bible, and his connection with the Manichees. There is also the vivid and memorable description of his sinfulness in Carthage, in which (perhaps surprising to us), actual sexual activity he seems to condemn with less abhorrence than he does his habit of viewing theatrical works onstage. He also mentions in passing his refusal to join a group of teenage vandals, "the wreckers":

> O Lord, I was a good deal quieter than the "wreckers" and kept well clear of their destructive activities. I was ashamed of the sense of shame that held me back from being like these "wreckers," whose perverse and diabolical nickname is almost a badge of good education; I associated with and sometimes enjoyed friendly contacts, but always recoiled from their acts of violence. They would chase sensitive freshmen relentlessly, taunting and hounding them on no provocation, simply for their own malicious amusement. Nothing is more like demonic activity than this behavior.[18]

If a sense of shame and propriety is all that keeps him from committing vandalism and terrorizing younger people, and not a real devotion to doing something noble or virtuous, then Augustine counts it as no virtue at all.

Book 4 returns to issues related to power, first directly, as Augustine describes how, as he had refrained from the senseless vandalism of the "wreckers," he also refuses to try to exercise power through sorcery, though as before, he finds his motives still insufficiently virtuous:

> Another thing I remember is that once when I had decided to enter a dramatic poetry contest some sorcerer fellow sent word to me to ask what was I prepared to pay him to ensure that I would win. I replied that I detested and loathed those obscene rites, and would not countenance the killing of a fly to bring me victory, even if the crown to be won were of gold that would last forever. This fellow was prepared to offer living creatures in sacrifice, and I suspected that he

---

[18]*Conf.* 3.3.6.

intended by these rites to enlist demonic support for my cause. But it was not out of reverence for your purity that I rejected this evil thing, O God of my heart, for I had not yet learned to love you; all I had learned was to think about brilliant material objects. Is not a soul that sighs for such make-believe gods wantonly forsaking you, trusting in illusions and feeding the winds? Yet while refusing to have sacrifice offered to demons on my behalf I was all the while offering myself in sacrifice to them through my superstition; for what does "feeding the winds" mean but feeding demons, providing pleasure and amusement for them by our errors?[19]

But even this seemingly pious restraint is not pure as to intent, Augustine claims years later as he is writing. If killing animals in some kind of ritual is too vulgar or wasteful for Augustine (or simply ineffective), it does not absolve him from the sinful desire to find some way to win empty praise and wealth. We moderns might praise someone who works hard to get money, and blame someone who steals it, and mock someone who buys huge quantities of scratch-off lottery tickets—focusing in each case on the means, not the ends. Augustine would blame all of the people listed for excessively loving and desiring a worthless thing (money), and not just how they are trying to obtain it in various ways (work, theft, or chance).

But with the next episode, the death of a friend, Augustine returns to another dynamic within friendship. In Book 2, he considered how the good of friendship could still have sinful results: qua friendship it is a human good, but in so far as the friends are pursuing together a sinful goal (theft), then doing so in a friendly and supportive manner doesn't cleanse the act of its sinfulness. Here in Book 4, he describes a much more poignant and insidious abuse of friendship for the sake of power: Augustine tries to tease a very close friend who had just received Catholic baptism while unconscious. But the friend is having none of it:

> How wrong I was; for he rallied and grew stronger, and immediately, or as soon as I possibly could (which is to say at the first moment he was fit for it, for I did not leave him, so closely were we dependent on each other), I attempted to chaff him, expecting him to join me in making fun of the baptism he had undergone while entirely absent in mind

---

[19]*Conf.* 4.2.3.

and unaware of what was happening. But he had already learned that he had received it, and he recoiled from me with a shudder as though I had been his enemy, and with amazing, new-found independence warned me that if I wished to be his friend I had better stop saying such things to him. I stood aghast and troubled, but deferred telling him of my feelings in order to let him get better first, thinking that once he was in normal health again I would be able to do what I liked with him. But he was snatched away from my mad designs, to be kept safe with you for my consolation: a few days later the fever seized him anew and he died. And I was not there.[20]

In the course of *Confessions*, Augustine will live with a woman out of wedlock for years, callously dump her, rush to form an advantageous engagement to a ten year old, cheat on her with another woman, teach what he finally believes are heresies, vainly and ambitiously try to rise in the ranks of academia by teaching others how to lie most effectively and convincingly, steal, lie to his saintly mother himself—but I don't think any of those are as damning as this line, "I would be able to do what I liked with him." Augustine is here admitting what he felt at the time: that he knew he was the cleverer and more dominant member of their relationship, and he was determined to intellectually bully and manipulate his friend—not discuss, not debate, not convince or convert or cajole, but just "do what I liked." And when the friend dies shortly thereafter, the crushing grief Augustine expresses is not just the pain of mortality and loss—it is guilt for having been such an arrogant bully, such a thoughtless, disrespectful lout—such a bad friend, in short;[21] or even, dread that he was incapable of true friendship.[22] If the previous episodes of infants and the pear tree showed the ubiquity of the *libido dominandi*,

---

[20]*Conf.* 4.4.8.
[21]Cf. James Wetzel, "The Trappings of Woe and Confessions of Grief," in *A Reader's Companion to Augustine's Confessions*, edited by Kim Paffenroth and Robert Kennedy (Louisville and London: Westminster John Knox, 2003) 53–69, esp. 62:

> Augustine did not of course owe his friend *belief* in the face of his friend's transfiguration, but he did owe it to the friendship not to dismiss out of hand what had elicited his friend's independence of heart and mind. It would have been enough had Augustine been willing to question his own self-certainties before his friend had to die. That is the sort of self-questioning we offer to someone, not out of respect for a superior argument, but out of love.

[22]Ibid., 63: "The madness in all this was that Augustine loved his friend on terms that made it impossible for him to have a friend."

this shows it needn't even include the thought or threat of physical force; as importantly, this shows that even at the time the events occurred, Augustine was conscious of his guilt. One cannot seek healing of a disease until one is aware one is stricken with it, as Augustine now is here.

These episodes (babies, pear tree, dead friend) are fundamental to any analysis of *Confessions*, but focusing on them now from the narrow and specific lens of "power" allows us to see more clearly how Augustine conceives of both sin and its cure. We could have lumped all of them under "Augustine's life of sin" or specified a bit more by calling it "pride," but then we would have missed the exact valence and implications included under "pride." As we have already hinted at: there is in Augustine's analyses of these episodes a relentless stripping away of other considerations or motives, sometimes the very motives we might have attributed to them as our first attempt to understand the meaning Augustine sees in these stories.[23] So it seems obvious, at first, that babies are overcome by their desire or need for food, but in the end, Augustine claims they are not driven to think and feel, "Mine!" at the life-giving milk, because they have plenty, and lose none by sharing. Augustine believes they really mean "Not yours!"—that it is not desire for sustenance that drives them, but desire for possession (and denial of another's rights).[24] Even more clear is the case of the pear theft, where young Augustine knows even at the time he commits it, he didn't want/need the pears, so there, "Mine!" can only mean "My act of theft," because there's nothing there that is really his, beyond being able to claim, "I did this, me, I'm in control!" And most poignantly and damnably, in his statement and analysis of grief, "My friend died," Augustine realizes with numbing horror that only grows the more he dwells on it, that the emphasis is on "*My* friend," not "My *friend*"—that the love was not for the friend, but for the possessing and commanding (even manipulating or dominating) him; and he was loved

---

[23]Cf. McInerney, *Greatness of Humility*, 56: "Although in his earliest works Augustine views evil as the source of sin, he later makes the transition to placing sin's origin in the disordered love of self he understands as pride."

[24]Brighter students who are paying attention, assure me during seminars on *Confessions*, that newborns cannot feel jealousy as Augustine describes. While I suppose this would undermine the doctrine of original sin being in us at birth, I have to wonder: How different would Augustine's analysis of sin and its pervasiveness be, if he had to modify his theory to be that we manifest sin at eighteen months, or two years, rather than at birth? It would seem to me, if he can plausibly diagnose sin at any time earlier than adolescence (i.e., earlier than it can be blamed on culture or socialization), he has made it "original" enough to support the conclusions he draws.

not for himself, but for how he could make Augustine feel, how he could bolster his self-esteem and self-importance—a trophy friend, if you will.

This helps us to see more fully, then, what is offered by the alternative. If sinful loves are not best understood as overwhelming desire for the beloved object or person, but for possession, this specifies how Christ is both the cure and the ultimate stumbling block,[25] as Augustine describes it in Book 7:

> I also read in them that God, the Word, was born not of blood nor man's desire nor lust of the flesh, but of God, but that the Word was made flesh and dwelt among us, I did not read there. I certainly observed that in these writings it was often stated, in a variety of ways, that the Son, being in the form of God the Father, deemed it no robbery to be equal to God, because he is identical with him in nature. But that he emptied himself and took on the form of a slave, and being made in the likeness of men was found in human form, that he humbled himself and was made obedient to the point of death, even death on a cross, which is why God raised him from the dead, and gave him a name above every other name, so that at the name of Jesus every knee should bow, in heaven, on earth, or in the underworld, and every tongue confess that Jesus Christ is Lord, in the glory of God the Father, of this no mention was made in these books.[26]

This specifies Christ's humility as not mere weakness but lack of possessiveness (even though, as God, everything is His) and refusal (not lack of ability) to exert power over others.[27] It also specifies the pride Augustine attributes to himself and "the Platonists," not as mere arrogance or superiority ("I'm smarter than you!"), but as the epitome of such possessiveness ("This knowledge is *mine!*"), that their brilliance is theirs, their own possession,

---

[25]Cf. Deborah Wallace Ruddy, "The Humble God: Healer, Mediator, and Sacrifice," *Logos: A Journal of Catholic Thought and Culture* 7.3 (2004) 87–108: 91 "The humbling of the Word simultaneously reveals the desperate state of humanity and the immense worth of humanity. God's extravagant self-emptying love revealed in the Incarnation highlights, by contrast, the possessiveness of human love."

[26]*Conf.* 7.9.14. Cf. Ruddy, "The Humble God," 99, quoting the same connection of the opening of the Gospel of John and the hymn from Philippians, in Augustine's Sermons.

[27]Cf. Kent Dunnington, "Humility: an Augustinian perspective," *Pro Ecclesia: A Journal of Catholic and Evangelical Theology* 25.1 (Winter 2016) 18–43, section 4, paragraph 8: "Here, Christ's humility is associated with his apparent relinquishment of what he could rightly lay claim to, in order to serve others. Self-expenditure and self-giving over against self-enclosure and self-possession are thus highlighted as expressions of the humility of Christ."

gained through their own effort.[28] They enjoy the act and feeling of possession rather than the knowledge itself, which leaves Augustine contemplating the irony of the situation: they are exalted and wise because they have such knowledge but that should make them humble (at such knowledge being graciously revealed).[29] The essence of sin is this claim of self-sufficiency and independence.[30] Christ's self-emptying (*kenosis*) is his sinlessness and his infinite (paradoxical) power.[31]

But how can such humility be expressed by humans other than Christ, since they do not possess his infinite power, they are not usually subject to death on a cross, and a paradox is not transparently exemplary but would

---

[28]Cf. Dunnington, "Humility," section 3, paragraph 16:

> Augustine therefore locates a quest for a secure and independent self-image at the heart of pagan virtue. This, he argues, is in fact the essence of superbia, the quest for a self-image that is secure even in the face of biological death--a kind of immortal identity--and a self-image that reflects self-sufficiency--a kind of identity that is free from any ultimate neediness.

Cf. Jane Foulcher, *Reclaiming Humility: Four Studies in the Monastic Tradition* (Collegeville, MN: Liturgical Press, 2015) 26–27: "Indeed, for Augustine, humility is the very quality that distinguishes Christianity from paganism." Also McInerney, *Greatness of Humility*, 51, 62: "Unlike his Greek and Roman predecessors, Augustine views the human person as created by and for the God of Jesus Christ… In addition, pride serves to subvert the very achievements of the pagan philosophers. As they develop virtue and the ability to temper their emotions, they become proud and exult in that virtue." Also Ruddy, "Humble God," 88: "In reference to the various moral systems of his day, Augustine writes, 'Everywhere are to be found excellent precepts concerning morals and discipline, but this humility is not to be found.'"

[29]Cf. McInerney, *Greatness of Humility*, 52: "Humans are images of God because they are illuminated by Christ's divine light." Also Ruddy, "Humble God," 91: "The humbling of the Word simultaneously reveals the desperate state of humanity and the immense worth of humanity." On the Greeks' failure to grasp this, see Schlabach, "Hermeneutic of Humility," 315–16: "His implicit critique of the neo-Platonists to whom he owed so much suggests that the moral problem is not neatly one of intellection versus will but something more complex—an unwillingness to follow through on the quest for truth even or especially when the quest finally implicates one's own self as willingly self-deceived."

[30]See Dunnington, "Humility," section 3, paragraph 2: "Thus for Augustine pride is not essentially the aspiration to greatness but rather the aspiration to independence and self-sufficiency."

[31]Cf. Ruddy, "The Humble God," 88, 90: "Christ's humility is a 'saving humility'. Moreover, the way God saves us is inseparable from salvation itself… Without losing what God is, God becomes what God is not. In Jesus Christ, a new kind of sublimity is introduced, a new way of seeing is discovered—lowliness is inseparable from grandeur; humility is inextricably tied to exaltation." Also Schlabach, "Hermeneutic of Humility," 316: "Confronting the weakened lowliness of the Godhead at our feet, where God had 'built for himself out of our clay a lowly dwelling', would heal and strengthen the will by weakening it."

need some explanation for most of us to apply it?[32] It seems, ultimately, to be straightforward enough to state, if difficult to practice. For Augustine, humility is giving an honest and truthful appraisal of ourselves and ceasing to cling to the delusion of self-sufficiency. As with other points of his analysis, Augustine believes pagan virtue had the right inclinations, but just didn't go far enough. Pagan virtue could acknowledge everyone is dependent in some ways on other people, but to achieve the kind of transparency and full disclosure that Augustine envisions here would be to embrace "radical dependence," even for one's identity, from God, and not created by oneself.[33] It would be to embrace a wholly different kind of death than the inevitable, biological one we all face, but a dying to the power of death, and thereby living in ways that partly resemble (or even lead to) biological death—living in relation (dependence), giving power to or living for others, and being receptive to the needs of others.[34]

Augustine's life as narrated in *Confessions* gives some examples of such practices to train oneself in such humility. Prayer is an illustration of radical dependence, even for one's identity, and it shapes the form of *Confessions*, which is told as an extended prayer, a communication with

---

[32]Further, the paradox goes back not just to Christ's divine power revealed in weakness but to Augustine's opening question of how even to begin the quest for God, which has its roots in Aristotle's theory of virtue. See Schlabach, "Hermeneutic of Humilty," 321: "It seems we must be virtuous to do virtuous acts, but must practice the virtues to become virtuous… In effect, Aristotle's answer was simply, *Yes, that's right*" (emphasis in original).

[33]Thus, Dunnington, "Humility," section 3, paragraph 16: "The Christian knows ultimately whatever it may mean to have a 'truthful self-image' it will include radical dependence on God, therefore the Christian trains herself not only to acknowledge her need for others (which the pagans also do) but even to embrace her ultimate neediness (which the pagans do not) because such neediness is the core of whatever a truthful self-image for her may be." Cf. Foulcher, *Reclaiming Humility*, 26: "Appropriating the Greek philosophical notion of *eudamonia*, Augustine recasts human flourishing or *beatitudo* (blessedness) as founded on the knowledge of God, with the goal or end of human life 'the enjoyment of God.'"

[34]Cf. Dunnington, "Humility," section 4, paragraph 10:

> The humility of Christ thus transfigures the relationship between the self and death. This, I suggest, is the meaning of the strange claim Augustine makes about the moments leading up to his final surrender: "I was hesitating whether to die to death and live to life" (8.11.25). What could it mean to die to death? Surely Christ is the exemplar here, he who was obedient even unto death. It was Christ who showed us how to "die to death." This of course does not mean that Christ does not die, rather it means he dies to the controlling power of death… This is possible only if there is another kind of selfhood, a selfhood that is not finally threatened by poverty and dying—inevitable risks of dependence—but rather that is sustained by relationality, self-expenditure, and needy receptivity.

God and entirely dependent on God to hear and answer it.[35] And within the narrative, Monica is an exemplar of humility expressed in prayer for Augustine.[36] Further, Monica not only provides an example of humble prayer: Augustine credits her and Ambrose with giving him instruction.[37] Simplicianus and Ponticianus exhort to humility by means of "narrative embodiment" (they tell exemplary stories, especially the story of Victorinus' conversion and baptism,[38] that Augustine passes on to us). And Augustine seems to have thrived on the kind of relationality or sociability that fosters humility—even if he gives the good, reasonable, philosophical justification that it (sociability) is conducive to contemplation or intellectual pursuits. He describes such relationships among the community members at Cassiciacum, and in his long-term friendships with Alypius and Nebridius.[39] All of these—prayer; instruction (catechesis); long, committed relationships encouraging meaningful conversations with friends and respectful debates with adversaries—foster humility or "radical dependence" in Augustine.

But let us pause a moment at the end of this chapter to examine how far we have come from the sinful exercise of power, and what obstacles Augustine left in his own path, and perhaps bequeathed even to us in our stumbling

---

[35]Cf. Dunnington, "Humility," section 3, paragraph 3:

> The form of the *Confessions* in general is meant to challenge the notion that we can truthfully tell the story of who we are—of our identities—abstracted from God. Thus the *Confessions* exemplifies Christian humility in its refusal to speak of the self except in the mode of prayer. It is not simply that Augustine needs to give thanks for what God has helped him discover and accomplish, rather Augustine does not believe there is a 'self' he can truthfully identify abstracted from its utter dependence on God.

Also Schlabach, "Hermeneutic of Humility," 321–2: "Augustine first posed the problem as a way of initiating himself *and others* into the habit of confession that would develop and strengthen a steadfast orientation of the self, the integration of intellect and emotion, in humility toward God" (emphasis in original).

[36]Cf. Michael Gladwin, "Embodying Humility in Augustine's Confessions," *St. Mark's Review* 256.2 (June/July 2021) 53–65, esp. 57: "Here, in the narrated life of Monica, is an embodiment of the fundamentally important practice of intercessory prayer, with its dependence on God and selfless focus on the good of others."

[37]See Gladwin, "Embodying Humility," 57–8.

[38]Thus Gladwin, "Embodying Humility," 58–9. See also Foulcher, *Reclaiming Humility*, 27–8.

[39]See Gladwin, "Embodying Humility," 59; also Foulcher, *Reclaiming Humility*, 27: "Further, for Augustine, the embrace of the humble way of Christ continues to have social consequences." As importantly, such humility embraces respect toward adversaries: see Schlabach, "Hermeneutic of Humility," 323, "Augustine himself linked nonviolence toward the truth to a corollary with respect to (and for) persons—Christians must be patient with their opponents so as to give them opportunity to repent."

progress. The scenes of abusive power that Augustine describes in Books 1 and 2 are almost too melodramatic, given their subject matter (babies and teenagers): that Augustine endows them with so much importance and anthropological baggage need not necessarily strike us as convincing so much as overwrought. As I've said most semesters about Augustine (or Lear): he is too extra. But the glimpse of real guilt in Book 4 should warn us that Augustine can be both withering in his self-evaluation, but also has tendencies so ingrained he may never have eradicated them completely. That he felt guilty over how he had treated his friend is an impressive moment of candor (we would not, after all, even be aware of what happened if he hadn't told us—it was a completely private moment). But we needn't therefore assume he has told us about everything we may find blameworthy. If Augustine is prone to bullying people as he did his friend (and who of us wouldn't succumb to such, if we were as bright and eloquent as Augustine?), then doesn't his attempt to discount and brush aside Monica's dream at the end of Book 3 (*Conf.* 3.11.19-20) seem rather like another example of Augustine the bully (even if she, like the friend, is strong and faithful enough to overcome his intimidation)? And perhaps worse than failed bullying is his successful lying to her so he can escape her nagging and get to Rome to pursue what he finds important at the time (*Conf.* 5.8.15)—ambition seems his besetting sin more than domination or lust (and should make us suspicious of how he steers his final analysis back to concupiscence, as we will see). His dismissal of the mother of his child so he can marry a wealthy ten year old (after waiting the requisite two years) is another unflattering admission (*Conf.* 6.15.25), related to his continuing to prioritize his upward mobility, that isn't much ameliorated by his feeling bad about it later: his ambition overruled his deep affection and care for another person. (And trying to blame Monica for that situation, given that he had just lied to her about his travel plans, seems less than fully honest, as pleasing her never seems plausibly to have been his main priority.) These scenes taken together leave us with the impression that Augustine's theorizing of the "radical dependence" shown in humbly serving others, only partly overcame his more ambitious and abusive exercise of power, and only after years of struggle. Further, that his most callous, uncaring, disrespectful acts that he records are directed at his own mother and the mother of his child (without the profound guilt he feels over disrespecting his friend in Book 4) makes it seem not incredible for us to gender our description: Augustine finds it easier to overlook the needs and feelings of women, than he would those of a male peer and use power in a selfish, abusive way against the women in his life.

CHAPTER 2
LEAR AND POWER

Having analyzed Augustine's development—from prideful use/abuse of power, to humble submission to God and service to other people—we now consider how similar Lear's development may be, and how it may go differently. To do so, it may help to begin with a related concept we did not consider directly with Augustine—humiliation—for insight into the process of learning humility, as in this quotation from an essay on Augustine that seems even more fitting in relation to Lear: "Sometimes it takes a lot of humiliation to learn a little humility."[1]

Unlike in *Confessions*, humiliation seems obvious throughout *King Lear*, and crucial to understanding the title character and what he goes through, from the opening interlude with Gloucester and his illegitimate son Edmund, whose dishonor begins in the Quarto with his being labelled as "Bastard" rather than his given name, and continues in any edition with his father Gloucester's flippant mockery of him and his "whore" mother (*King Lear* 1.1.24). The humiliation then transfers to the Lear family, with the king springing the announcement on his daughters that they must publicly proclaim their love for him, in front of all the assembled court. Although Goneril and Regan come up with glib, flattering speeches on the fly, even their lines can be delivered in such a way so as to show their shock and surprise at such a demand. Even if the bestowal of the kingdom was done to honor them, their father puts them through a humiliating spectacle to "earn" it, thereby negating any generosity and replacing it with conditions or obligations.[2] The whole setup is also further embarrassing to Goneril

---

[1] Ruddy, "Humble God," 87.
[2] Thus Stella Achilleos, "Sovereignty, Social Contract, and the State of Nature in King Lear," in *The Routledge Companion to Shakespeare and Philosophy*, edited by Craig Bourne and Emily Caddick Bourne (London: Routledge, 2019), 267–78, esp. 270: "[W]hat appears to be a radical act of gift-giving is in fact a non-gift as it carries with it the old king's own terms and conditions." See also Brian Sheerin, "Making Use of Nothing: The Sovereignties of King Lear," *Studies in Philology* 110.4 (2013): 789–811, esp. 802: "For Lear, the magnificent bestowal of land is clearly not only a means for him to 'unburden himself' of responsibility but also precisely a means to burden others with love and obligation through the familial bond of affection; there

and Regan by Lear announcing explicitly that Cordelia is his favorite and the whole thing is rigged to give her the better share. Though with her two asides, Cordelia seems more clearly nonplussed by the scene: such "favor" is not experienced by her as positive. She is then explicitly shamed by her father cursing and disowning her, a humiliation he then also directs at his honest and faithful servant, Kent, with banishment and threat of execution. The scene ends with the Lear daughters exchanging barbed comments, deriding one another's supposed virtues as hidden vices of which they should be ashamed.

Thus, the first scene of the play sees several characters humiliated, most of them so by Lear. But the remainder of Act 1 and all of Act 2 show a transition, from humiliation heaped on the servants, Kent (being put in the stocks) and Oswald (tripped and subsequently insulted and beaten by Kent), to increasingly overt and unpunished humiliation directed at Lear by Goneril and Regan. Lear's humiliation increases in Act 3, and after the initial barring of him outdoors, it even ceases to be from his daughters but becomes almost cosmic with the description of the seemingly unprecedented and apocalyptic storm that Lear suffers in the humiliating state of increasing nakedness. It also becomes physiological and psychological for Lear, as he loses both his mental and physical integrity and vitality, driven to prancing about uttering gibberish, or unconscious and unable to respond. He is joined in this ordeal by his godson, Edgar, dressed in rags and feigning madness, and Gloucester, blinded by Cornwall and now wandering about with bloody rags over his eyes. After some false hope of such humiliation being stopped, reversed, and avenged in Act 4, Lear (along with most of the rest of the cast) suffers the humiliation of death, made far worse for him by his realization that all of this was brought about by his own actions at the beginning of the play.

This rehearsal of the play, focusing on humiliation, shows that the concept is vividly depicted in most of the action of the play and moves quickly and decisively from Lear humiliating others to him being humiliated (first by Goneril and Regan, then by the universe itself). But how or whether Lear learns humility, and what kind of humility he might learn, will occupy us for the rest of this chapter because it is not so obvious. In other words, in the terms of analyzing tragedy, Lear's mistake or flaw (hamartia) is clear in the opening scene, as is his fall or reversal of fortune (peripeteia) in the following acts, from a powerful, respected, and feared king to a nearly naked homeless

---

is no doubt that Lear believes he has sealed a long term pact precisely by means of permanently indebting others."

man, who can be ignored or reviled with impunity; further, he has caused the deaths of everyone he loves and the destruction of the kingdom. To what extent he experiences a full realization (anagnorisis) of this (beyond "This happened because of things I did") is less obvious. Someone may feel bad for what happened (e.g., "It's too bad I stepped out into traffic without seeing the bus careening down the street towards me, and thereby got run over and died") without full acceptance of guilt, blame, or responsibility and without learning a better way to behave; it may also be (and it is perfectly compatible with tragedy), that although the protagonist's actions contribute to their downfall, such actions may have been unavoidable. Even if Lear comes to a realization, what he realizes may be very different or even incompatible with the humility we have seen in Augustine's *Confessions*, so we must make our comparison and draw our connections very carefully and precisely.

Returning to the beginning of the play and focusing on how characters use or react to power, Lear begins by giving power away (which ironically, seems to be meant by him as his most powerful act).[3] Taking Lear at his word, he describes power in completely negative terms: it is not desirable but is just "cares and business" (*King Lear* 1.1.41, repeating "cares" at 1.1.55). Giving it away will make Lear "unburdened" (*King Lear* 1.1.43).[4] But drawing out the implications of "care": power is a burden to Lear, filling him with cares and concerns that he'd rather not have because he does not care about power.[5] So far this would not necessarily imply a prideful abuse of power (it might seem rather the opposite) but by the end of Lear's first speech, building on

---

[3] Cf. Achilleos, "Sovereignty, Social Contract," 268: "Ironically, little does Lear realize how—far from confirming his absolute sovereignty—his 'radical bestowal' or 'potlatch', the distribution of all of his lands, actually negates his sovereignty, reducing him, as Sheerin argues, to a 'nothing.'" For Sheerin's argument, see Brian Sheerin, "Making Use of Nothing: The Sovereignties of *King Lear*," *Studies in Philology* 110.4 (2013): 789–811, esp. 790: "In depicting Lear as giving away his kingdom as a series of lavish presents, furthermore, the text diligently highlights a trajectory toward nothingness that begins as gift bestowal."

[4] Though cf. Marianne Novy, *Love's Argument: Gender Relations in Shakespeare* (Chapel Hill: University of North Carolina Press, 1984), 152: "Lear's childishness has been noted by many critics of the play, as well as the Fool and, self-interestedly, Goneril—'Old fools are babes again' (1.3.19); but it has been less observed that the similarity between king and child is in part in their assumptions of omnipotence encouraged—for different reasons—by the flattery of those who care for them." Also cf. the tyranny of babies described in Chapter 2 above in *Confessions*.

[5] The protagonist disastrously giving away power occurs in several Shakespeare plays. See Stephen Greenblatt, *Shakespeare's Freedom* (Chicago: University of Chicago Press, 2010), 81: "What all of these very different characters have in common … is the desire to escape from the burdens of governance. In each case, the desire leads to disaster."

another aspect or meaning of "care" unfortunately takes him right to the heart of pride and tyranny, by connecting the removal of his own cares, with a display of love, or care, for him: "Which of you shall we say doth love us most, / That we our largest bounty may extend / Where nature doth with merit challenge" (*King Lear* 1.1.56-8). Lear may not value power over the kingdom, but he seems here rather grotesquely to value exerting power over his daughters,[6] by forcing them to show everyone how much they care for/love him.

Lear's daughters in their different ways all focus not on the power/submission of Lear's demand but that it is a command to speak ("Speak," *King Lear* 1.1.59, 75, 95, 99), that will lead to the commander responding in speech ("Which of you shall we say"), so they focus on speech. Goneril gives the unremarkable (and if her deeds did not subsequently prove otherwise, believable) claim that speech is not adequate to express such profound love as she supposedly feels: "I love you more than word can wield the matter" (*King Lear* 1.1.60-1). Regan brings in a different kind of hyperbole, implying that her love transcends speech and could only be properly expressed through deeds: "In my true heart I find she names my very deed of love" (*King Lear* 1.1.77-8). The phrasing, however, verges on the incestuous, and as with Goneril, her subsequent deeds belie the fantasy she paints here for her father. But she does raise the "heart" as the right locus of feelings, which Cordelia then picks up on and elaborates without any incestuous implications: "I cannot heave My heart into my mouth" (*King Lear* 1.1.100-1). Cordelia does not simply assert the inadequacy of speech (Goneril), or imply sex would be a better, fuller love language if it were allowed (Regan): she asserts the superiority, even ineffability or holiness of her heart over any of the rest of her.[7]

But this statement of hers only comes after the repeated, "Nothing" (*King Lear* 1.1.96, 98). Although Cordelia can give a response like her sisters', and address the issue of speech, that is not her real response. Her first two responses, then, are not to declare the heart's elevated, pristine status (which

---

[6] Cf. Achilleos, "Sovereignty, Social Contract," 267: "The opening scene … emphasizes Lear's majesty and sovereign power."

[7] Cf. Kenneth J. E. Graham, "'Without the Form of Justice': Plainness and the Performance of Love in *King Lear*," *Shakespeare Quarterly* 42.4 (Winter 1991): 438-61, esp. 443: "By failing to speak as Lear commands, she offends the law, yet she implies (without appearing to understand fully her own implications) that an exception should be made in her case because her silent conviction possesses a degree of certainty greater than any that the spoken forms of the present law can reach."

she only does under the further demands/threats of her father) but to refuse the command at all—not to speak in a certain (correct) way, but simply not to speak, except for two syllables issuing a refusal to speak. The exact meaning behind this refusal or defiance is debatable, perhaps even finally mysterious, but I don't think is crucial for understanding the dynamics and what it does to Lear's self-understanding: why his one daughter does not humor him is unclear, but that she doesn't, and that Lear finds it intolerable, is completely unambiguous.[8] And further—it is probably most accurate to say Lear finds Cordelia incomprehensible at this point (cf. Goneril and Regan, who are speaking in terms he can understand, but he knows they're lying).[9] But the revealing part is that Lear finds an enigmatic but truthful beloved much more intolerable than someone he knows is lying because the liar seems to fit into his preconceived plans of how the world ought to work (i.e., with him in charge).[10] As we saw with Augustine, Lear demands a beloved who is uniform and predictable, acting as he demands, or can be manipulated into such. This is what lies behind Lear's outward claims of devaluing and disposing of power: with the "love contest" and his reaction to Cordelia's "wrong" answer, he shows what kind of power he really wanted over his daughters. Again, whether the unpredictability Cordelia displays is from youthful rebellion, or idealistic honesty, or alterity, or heteronomy, accepting such is in the essence of really loving someone, and not just loving an extension or duplicate of oneself—that is, an idol.[11] So as Lear reacts to Cordelia's unexpected (non-)response (Goneril and Regan's seem completely predicted and unimpressive to him), Lear frames her response in terms he can understand—in modern language, he projects what would be his feelings, if he had given her response. He calls her "untender" (*King*

---

[8] Mehrdad Bidgoli, "Ethics, Subjectivity, and Alterity in *King Lear*: On Cordelia's Defiance and Sacrifice," *Religion and the Arts: A Journal from Boston College* 25.4 (2021): 385–420, offers an analysis of Cordelia in which I think the disconnect between her and her father remains, regardless of how we label her: "her absolute heteronomy, sensibility, and receptivity—which posits her beneath and prior to Lear's onto-political system" ("Ethics, Subjectivity," 395).
[9] Cf. Bidgoli, "Ethics, Subjectivity," 403, 404: "Goneril and Regan inhabit Lear's onto-political order … If Lear is astonished, one reason is that he cannot locate Cordelia within his order."
[10] Cf. Bidgoli, "Ethics, Subjectivity," 398: "The way Lear turns to his daughters is quite intentional, as if they are phenomena to be mastered over and reduced to knowledge, seeing love also as an object to be addressed and incarnated via and within their rhetoric."
[11] Cf. Bidgoli, "Ethics, Subjectivity," 402: "Lear thus excitedly wants his daughters to 'heave' their real feelings to their tongues but instead only turns them into assimilatory extensions of himself."

Lear 1.1.118), and most significantly, he says she is acting out of "pride" (*King Lear* 1.1.145)—when of course the whole scene was arranged by him to satisfy his pride, vanity, self-importance, and neediness.[12] And now that he is not satisfied (obeyed), he'll blame that on her supposed pride.[13]

In our first volume, we considered Cordelia's response in relation to the play's ideas on "love" but here we'll stay with the related issue of power. Cordelia's response is not sufficiently subservient for Lear, but is there a deeper conflict with regards to power and submission here (rather than just noting, as in our previous work, that there is confusion and lack of communication on "love")? Is it that Cordelia and her father cannot agree on love because their conflict is based on unstated assumptions about power, just expressed in words about love? Both have a subtext, in other words, that is the basis of their conflict but is so hidden from/by both that they're shouting about other issues to obscure what is really going on. When Cordelia finally gets to an answer roughly analogous to her sisters' and to what Lear demanded, it is clearly rational and without emotion (even if the actor is sobbing, as she usually is at that point in the scene). It is without hyperbole or sentimentality, so it is accurate (and limited) within the terms it sets itself. And these are not the terms of what she feels, or values, but simply what has been done for her, and what she then does in response—that is, she speaks in terms of the exercise of reciprocal powers: "I love your Majesty According to my bond, no more nor less ... You have begot me, bred me, loved me. I return those duties back as are right fit" (*King Lear* 1.1.101-2, 106-7). Cordelia describes "love" as the fulfillment of obligations, flowing from the beloved having fulfilled those of the bond from the other side.[14] It is

---

[12]Cf. Harold Bloom, *Shakespeare: The Invention of the Human* (New York: Riverhead Books, 1998), 508: "It is fascinating that Lear initially attributes Cordelia's recalcitrance to join in her sisters' pompous hyperboles to 'pride, which she calls plainness'. Lear and all three daughters suffer from a plethora of prides."

[13]Cf. Graham, "Without the Form of Justice," 444-5:

> With this accusation of pride, Lear voices a common criticism of private plainness: the person who rejects public forms is saying they are not good enough for him or her, thus implying that he or she is too good for them ... The claim to sincerity, to a uniquely outward inwardness, Lear suggests, is a fraud, indicating nothing other than the deadliest sin, pride.

[14]See Jerry Wasserman, "'And Every One Have Need of Other': Bond and Relationship in King Lear," *Mosaic: An Interdisciplinary Critical Journal* 9.2 (Winter 1976): 15-30, esp. 17: "Their [Barish and Waingrow] main concern is with the reciprocal nature of the bond of service, 'where privileges are granted at the same time that duties are imposed.'"

mathematical and mercantile; if Cordelia were struggling to say something that wasn't sentimental or trite, she needn't have picked something so utterly devoid of passion.[15] And again, as powerful and extensive as such a "bond" and its exercise may be, it is limited. Whereas Goneril and Regan's answers kept stating in their various ways, "More! More!" Cordelia's is "Just this much, no more"—and in response to a demand for absolute submission, following on Lear's surrender of "all" to them, this answer seems incommensurate, even meager, in terms of power (never mind in terms of emotion, which may well be part of Lear's agenda/assumption).[16] Further, as mathematical as it may seem in Cordelia's telling, it is also not just an equation with several variables, but many equations with many variables, for all people simultaneously participate in many of these reciprocal bonds, which have various and competing duties.[17]

Cordelia then unpacks this further, and more disastrously, by asserting such "love" is not just finite, it is divisible (into ever decreasing chunks,

---

[15]Cf. Alex Schulman, *Rethinking Shakespeare's Political Philosophy: From Lear to Leviathan* (Edinburgh: Edinburgh University Press, 2014), 103: "Lear requiring a literal demonstration of love, spoken not in a setting of private intimacy but in public, feels strange. But given the context it is arguably less strange than Cordelia's reply that love is contractual, even mathematical."

[16]Cf. Wasserman, "And Every One Have Need," 18:

> But Shakespeare's stress is on the limited, mathematical sense of the reciprocity entailed in Holinshed's version: so much for so much ... The quid pro quo quality of this bond, as Cordelia understands it, recognizes its reciprocal nature but severely delimits the rights and obligations of both parties. The situation, the sense, the balanced phrasing, and the strict one-to-one ratio of everything in Cordelia's speech reveal methodical calculation. In context the word 'bond' even takes on legalistic overtones.

[17]Cf. Wasserman, "And Every One Have Need," 17:

> Each character appears, depending on the circumstances, in one or another or a multiplicity of his roles simultaneously ... Each role determines a relationship and each relationship has its bond. In order for a character to properly demand the rights due him and carry out the obligations he owes, he must distinguish his various roles and understand the bonds belonging to each of the relationships growing out of these roles.

And while it seems clear that there is confusion between these roles, even in the analysis, critics seem unable to decide whether Cordelia is misconstruing her duties as a daughter, or as a subject, as in Wasserman's subsequent analysis ("And Every One Have Need," 18–29):

> But within the framework of the father-child relationship her understanding of the bond, though perhaps excessively judicious, is perfectly correct ... Her error lies in understanding the bond between herself and Lear only in terms of child and father ... But for the daughter of the king to circumscribe her relationship as severely as Cordelia does is a serious breach of ethics.

with each subsequent partition): "That lord whose hand must take my plight shall carry Half my love with him, half my care and duty" (*King Lear* 1.1.111–13).[18] If Regan took the hyperbole in the direction of incest ("my very deed of love … an enemy to all other joys" [*King Lear* 1.1.78–80]), Cordelia also takes it there, in terms of directly connecting the filial bond with the marital bond, equating husband and father as both receiving portions of her "care and duty" (and thereby repeating the word Lear used, "care," to describe his power and what he was handing over to his daughters).[19] With this analysis, Lear's rage is not from confusing and equating obedience and love but from taking literally Cordelia's implication here, that the power she recognizes and honors in her father is steadily decreasing throughout her life (as she takes on further bonds, such as a husband, and then with the begetting of children). Lear's pride, therefore, is not about being emotionally needy or sentimental (though it is satisfied by Goneril and Regan's appeals to sentimentality) but by needing his absolute power uniquely recognized and submitted to (even though he is the one who began the process of dividing his power) and without a rival—that is, tyrannical jealousy. Of course, one can imagine Cordelia not phrasing either love or duty in such divisible terms, or Lear accepting such a description: if her father needs reassurance of his continued power/relevance, she could remind him her betrothal forges an important alliance, extending his power, not diminishing it, and future children of the Lear line will continue that expansion. In other words, Cordelia here presents and Lear explodes at the idea that power dilutes with time and the addition of more partners/bonds, but such an analysis is neither necessary nor inevitable. It may even be that Cordelia's answer here shows some family resemblance by asserting her power over her father (or at least

---

[18] And it is Lear's dividing of his power, not the handing over, that is the real problem: see Achilleos, "Sovereignty, Social Contract," 269–70, "What Lear appears to be strikingly blind to in dividing his lands between his daughters is what Shakespeare's near-contemporary French jurist and political philosopher Jean Bodin described as the indivisibility of sovereign power …. This multiple fracturing of sovereign power suggests an element of political naivete, or political schizophrenia, as we could perhaps venture to call it."

[19] With the incest airbrushed out, see Wasserman, "And Every One Have Need," 18: "And with Cordelia's choice of the same terms that comprise the marriage vow – 'obey', 'love', and 'honor' – she is saying that her bond with her father is no less sacred nor serious than the holy bond of marriage." Also cf. Bloom, *Invention of the Human*, 508: "Freud most peculiarly thought that Lear burned with repressed lust for Cordelia, perhaps because the great analyst did for his Anna."

willfully refusing his power to make her speak as he desires), as he insists on imposing his will on his daughters.[20]

In Lear's subsequent cursing of Cordelia and division of his kingdom between Goneril and Regan (and their husbands), Kent intervenes, and he too picks up on the language of "duty" and the idea of reciprocal obligations. He begins by enumerating all the roles that Lear fulfills in his life, and to which he has faithfully responded: "Royal Lear, Whom I have ever honored as my king, Loved as my father, as my master followed, As my great patron thought on in my prayers" (*King Lear* 1.1.156-9). He moves on to the most extreme and graphic illustration of such loyalty—the willingness to lay down his life for his king: "Let it fall rather, though the fork invade the region of my heart" (*King Lear* 1.1.161-2, with a further echo of Cordelia's invocation of the sanctity of the subject's "heart"). But the point Lear cannot tolerate in his servant is when Kent then includes as a "duty" that he must contradict his king: "Think'st thou that duty shall have dread to speak When power to flattery bows?" (*King Lear* 1.1.164-5). Lear's pride dictates that his power cannot be contradicted, but Kent here shows that in fact it is a supreme act of loyalty to save his king from his own folly, and even one that is dictated and reinforced by all the roles Lear fulfills in his life.[21] Real respect for Lear's power includes devotion to the truth,[22] which would ultimately protect and maintain his master's

---

[20]Cf. Wasserman, "And Every One Have Need," 18: "As Coleridge and others have noted, there is in her speech 'something of disgust at the ruthless hypocrisy of her sisters, some little faulty admixture of pride and sullenness.'"

[21]Cf. Matthew M. Davis, "'My Master Calls Me': Authority and Loyalty in *King Lear*," *Renascence* 70.1 (Wint 2018): 59-78, esp. 69: "Kent not only expresses his own view that Lear is acting foolishly, he also makes it clear that he is acting in accordance with Duty, embracing his responsibility as a good counselor to the king"; cf. Wasserman, "And Every One Have Need," 25-6:

> By Intervening on Cordelia's behalf, Kent has violated – in Lear's eyes – his bond of allegiance to both the King and the man, his master and the father of Cordelia ... There is a fulness and lucidity about Kent that contrasts markedly in the opening scene with the narrow exclusiveness of Cordelia's filial duty and Lear's utter confusion ... His 'plainness' of speech is necessitated by his duty to Lear's majesty ... He is also bound to speak plainly by his love for Lear, his "father" ... Finally, it is the duty of service to his master that motivates Kent's behavior, here and throughout the play.

[22]Cf. Graham, "Without the Form of Justice," 445: "He thus appeals to the many traditions that support the aggressive aspect of private plainness. Privilege here has roughly the root sense of private law ... What supports such a privilege is partly the sense that any conviction certain enough to motivate anger and the desire for revenge in an honorable man is likely to be true."

well-being, but Lear only defines his own power as an arbitrary exercise of will, regardless of its outcomes. And significantly for our analysis, this exchange provides a balance, with Lear erupting in rage against a loving, loyal man, as he did with Cordelia; Lear's more gendered pride (that we also saw with Augustine) will be clearer in later scenes but for now his pride is an equal opportunity destroyer of his relationships.[23]

Following this, Lear is then under the care and control of Goneril and Regan, but he tries to maintain his power and prestige with a hundred knights under his (and not his daughters') command. He issues commands that are either ignored or not followed quickly enough (according to him). Into this situation, Kent returns in disguise and offers to serve Lear:

LEAR Dost thou know me, fellow?
KENT No, sir, but you have that in your countenance which I would fain call master.
LEAR What's that?
KENT Authority.

(*King Lear* 1.4.27–31)

Kent claims "authority" is still detectable in the former king, and it must be obeyed by a "honest-hearted fellow" (*King Lear* 1.4.20) such as himself.[24] And anyone, like Oswald, who does not recognize such innate authority, is a "clotpole" (*King Lear* 1.4.47) and a "knave ... whoreson dog ... slave ... cur" (*King Lear* 1.4.80–1); such a person can and should be beaten by Lear and Kent with license. The conception of Kent and Lear is that power (belonging to anyone who fulfills any of the roles Kent listed in the opening scene—king, father, master, patron) is not just granted or recognized by the governed, it is intrinsic and innate, and if it is not proclaimed by others, everything based on such relationships—kingdom, society, family,

---

[23]Kent's role of telling Lear truths he does not want to hear also corresponds roughly to a male vassal fulfilling the role that Monica does for Augustine.
[24]Cf. Davis, "'My Master Calls Me,'" 60–3:

> Kent, more than anyone else in the play, ... is guided by a conception of Lear as someone who is *inherently different* from other men, someone who possesses an innate, indefeasible authority ... There is, literally, no situation in which Lear can be placed that will cause him to seem un-kingly to Kent because Kent views Lear as *inherently* kingly.

(emphasis original)

apparently even the cosmos—disintegrates into chaos.[25] Such power is not conventional, accidental, or temporary but an "elemental force,"[26] the glue that holds together society and the universe.

It is in this scene that Lear's exercise of power is revealed as gendered because to Goneril's refusal to recognize his authority, and her attack on it by dismissing half of his retinue, Lear unleashes a barrage of grotesque curses against her—"degenerate bastard" (*King Lear* 1.4.263), "detested kite" (*King Lear* 1.4.274), and "wolvish visage" (*King Lear* 1.4.325). His attacks are even aimed at her specifically as a woman: "dry up in her the organs of increase, And from her derogate body never spring A babe to honor her. If she must teem, Create her child of spleen, that it may live And be a thwart disnatured to her" (*King Lear* 1.4.293-7). But to his son-in-law, Albany, Lear is deferential, almost apologetic (as he is subsequently to his other son-in-law, Cornwall). We will elaborate on this dynamic in a later chapter.

Furthering this theme, it is worth noting that many productions of the play have Oswald depicted on stage as very effeminate, so that even the contrast between good servant (Kent) and bad servant (Oswald) is enacted as male versus female(ish). But also noteworthy is the frequent double casting of Cordelia and the Fool, which we noted in our first volume, as it questions both how and to whom Lear's power is recognized and obeyed. Because with or without the double casting, the Fool is usually portrayed as unconventional as to gender (androgynous, hermaphroditic, or non-binary—I have seen him once on stage as an old drag queen),[27] and he is certainly unconventional in how he talks to Lear, with most of what he says far more mocking and less respectful than what got Kent banished in the opening scene. By his interactions with the Fool here, we get some hint (to be elaborated on during the storm scenes) that Lear can display very different ideas and attitudes about threats to his power, other than his typical (and most violently and acutely aimed at females) outrage.[28]

---

[25] On this, Kent is more consistent than even Lear himself: see Davis, "'My Master Calls Me,'" 63, "Kent is actually more consistent in his insistence on Lear's authority than Lear himself. After his experience on the heath, Lear begins to question the basis of his own authority, and indeed of authority in general."

[26] Sheerin, "Making Use of Nothing," 801.

[27] Bloom, *Invention of the Human*, 494, calls him "the uncanniest character in Shakespeare."

[28] Cf. Bloom, *Invention of the Human*, 510, where he identifies the character's emotion with his usual accuracy but sidesteps the gendered implications: "Mortality is the ultimate outrage we all of us must endure."

Augustine's Confessions and Shakespeare's King Lear

The confrontation between Lear and his two elder daughters continues and reaches its climax in Act 2, scene 4, first with Regan, and then with both daughters. One way to see the essence of the conflict is in Lear's simple line, "I gave you all" (*King Lear* 2.4.286), which can be variously delivered as shouted or whispered with equal effect—because whether Lear is enraged or stunned by what his daughters are doing, the problem is that he is unable to comprehend the difference between what he expected (assumed) would be the reaction and result of his giving away all his power (gratitude and reciprocal generosity), and what he is actually presented with (increasing hostility and denial of any power or autonomy to him).[29] The daughters' diminution of Lear's band of followers reaches its climax a few lines later, with Regan's line (like Lear's above, all monosyllables), "What need one?" (*King Lear* 2.4.303—again, delivered with various levels of energy—shrieking or quietly condescending—but full of hatred, venom, and menace, either way).

There follows a long and significant speech from Lear before he flees out into the storm. The ostensible topic of the preceding argument between Lear and his daughters has been how many followers Lear should have with him as he shuffles between their two castles. All this is only indirectly related to Lear's power, but the connection between one's material possessions and one's power unfolds in what follows. Lear's point has been that he deserves the number he appointed (one hundred)—anything less is disrespect, if it is done on the authority of others and over his objection. Goneril and Regan move the conversation in a very different direction—how many followers does Lear *need*? Or put another way—what are the reasons, for and against, any particular number of followers? And between those two very different ways of framing the question, there really is no connection or way to adjudicate—they are talking about the same issue (number of followers) but in completely different terms (respect and logic or necessity). Lear finally erupts at this incommensurability, with, "O reason not the need!" (*King Lear* 2.4.304), rightly noting that the reasons put forth by his daughters do not positively address his needs.

Lear follows this outburst with a very well-reasoned argument, but one from analogy, not strict logic. (It is also, ultimately, a very tightly packed

---

[29]Cf. Achilleos, "Sovereignty, Social Contract," 268: "He remains equally blind to how the distribution of all of his lands to his children renders him completely vulnerable: the body natural, stripped of the body politic, remains completely powerless, prey to the whims of those newly invested with power." Also Davis, "My Master Calls Me," 59: "Those who view authority as something defeasible are prepared to accept radical revisions in terms of the status and prestige accorded to individual persons over time."

piece of foreshadowing, before Lear begins his journey into beggary, nakedness, and finally madness.) He starts with a very general observation of human nature: "Our basest beggars are in the poorest thing superfluous. Allow not nature more than nature needs, man's life is cheap as beast's" (*King Lear* 2.4.304-7). Even beggars are not really reduced to barest essentials: they carry some object that has value to them other than its ability to help them survive, physically, and he protests his own reduction to such a state of merely being allowed to live.[30] Whether the particular object of the individual person has aesthetic or sentimental value doesn't matter and isn't specified: his point is, it has a value assigned to it by a human(s), not by the animal needs of hunger, thirst, warmth, protection from predators, or need to reproduce. It has value to a particular human, by showing what all humans deserve—respect for their particularity and individuality. But all this is very condensed and very removed (so far) from their present situation in a well-appointed castle, and all still nominally following the rules of decorum. So Lear moves his argument to address Regan directly, "Thou art a lady; If only to go warm were gorgeous, Why, nature needs not what thou gorgeous wear'st, Which scarcely keeps thee warm" (*King Lear* 2.4.307-10). To ask how many followers Lear needs, should be analogous to asking his princess/duchess daughters how many dresses or shoes they "need" because "need" here is defined not by how much they need protection from the elements but by what message their clothes need to convey.[31] Their clothes are to broadcast, "The wearer is an important, powerful, wealthy lady"; Lear needs the number of followers requisite to communicate that he is an important, respected, and (at least formerly) powerful man,[32] and he has set the number at 100 and it cannot be changed by someone else without communicating that Lear is not respected or powerful.

---

[30]Cf. Schulman, *Rethinking Shakespeare's Political Philosophy*, 110: "Lear equates reduction from locus of command to object of caretaking not merely to feminisation, but to animalisation."
[31]See (with historic precedents) Thelma Nelson Greenfield, "The Clothing Motif in *King Lear*," *Shakespeare Quarterly* 5.3 (1954): 281-6, esp. 284: "Regan is reminded that her dress is a part of her station."
[32]Cf. Daniel Juan Gil, *Shakespeare's Anti-Politics: Sovereign Power and the Life of the Flesh* (London: Palgrave Macmillan, 2013), 101:

> According to Lear, the bare life of man is in fact cheap as beast's, except for the superficial uniforms that society (embodied in the sovereign) puts on that life – a retinue of knights in the case of Lear, a fancy gown in the case of Goneril and Regan. Persons are made by the social roles they inhabit and carry out; the social role alone confers dignity and status as a person.

Lear moves on to enumerate the personal qualities he will need in order to endure the disrespect his daughters now heap on him. He begins with "patience" (*King Lear* 2.4.312) and connects it to his first painfully honest evaluation of himself—a description that simply lists the ways in which he now lacks power: "You see me here, you gods, a poor old man As full of grief as age, wretched in both" (*King Lear* 2.4.313–14). His evaluation is not just honest, it is surprisingly limited, given what a hyperbolic drama queen Lear is in nearly every other line of the play:[33] he simply states the obvious, that he is "a poor old man" and now "wretched." He invokes the gods—but not to avenge him (yet—more on that below), but again, just noting their presence and witness of his present state. It may be the only line in the play where Lear could be described as resigned rather than outraged, defiant, or despairing.

But this very brief reverie of patience is momentary because it is still so focused on Lear himself. Brief, limited self-pity may be better than explosive, enraged, expansive self-pity; but it is still just self-pity and not humility. And here it reverts to Lear's more typical reactions: blame of others (his daughters and the gods—*King Lear* 2.4.315–16) and rage (*King Lear* 2.4.317). It is again gendered—first with an inhuman restraint and denial of weeping at what he feels because Lear conceives of it as emasculating (*King Lear* 2.4.318–19),[34] degenerating into sputtering, incoherent threats against Goneril and Regan specifically as women:[35] "No, you unnatural hags, I will have such revenges on you both That all the world shall—I will do such things—What they are yet I know not, but they shall be The terrors of the

---

[33] Cf. Bloom, *Invention of the Human*, 493–4:

> Lear, beyond us in grandeur and in essential authority, is still a startlingly intimate figure, since he is an emblem of fatherhood itself. Outrageously hyperbolical, insanely eloquent, Lear nevertheless always demands more love than can be given (within the limitations of the human), and so he scarcely can speak without crossing into the realm of the unsayable.

[34] Cf. Daniel Juan Gil, *Shakespeare's Anti-Politics: Sovereign Power and the Life of the Flesh* (London: Palgrave Macmillan, 2013), esp. 104, where he goes further and claims it is not just emasculating but is undermining Lear's personhood: "These tears are not an expression of a true, emotional core self. Rather, Lear experiences them as an animated, alien life that has seized the surfaces of his body to produce non-self fluid, and he threatens to pluck his eyes out to stop this process, which feels like it is undermining his personhood from below or from within."

[35] Though the recent Branagh production of *King Lear* projects Lear's stammering further back into the scene and climaxes it here with Lear collapsing in a seizure. With such a depiction, it would not seem accurate to talk of Lear's point of view or his attitude, as we are just witnessing him succumbing to a physical malady.

earth!" (*King Lear* 2.4.319-23). Lear longs for the power he gave away in the first scene—that he said then he spurned, but now he sees its desirability; its memory is now so distant, however, that he can't even articulate what he would do with it if he did still have it. (Cf. his curse of Goneril in Act 1, scene 4, where Lear is his usual eloquent self at calling down gendered horrors of sterility, spleen, and tears—all feminine and maternal equivalents, to his mind, of the emasculation he has suffered as a man and father, from both daughters.) Now he can only turn his anger against his own tears (*King Lear* 2.4.324), his own heart (*King Lear* 2.4.325-6), and finally his own mind (*King Lear* 2.4.327). Ironically, the more vehemently and specifically Lear tries to direct his (now non-existent) power against women, the more powerfully self-destructive he becomes.

In the justly famous storm scenes that follow, Lear's attitude toward power changes, and the play's depiction of humility emerges. Lear begins this part of the play fully and suddenly regaining his eloquence he had lost in his final confrontation with Goneril and Regan. The wrongs they have done him are still part of his calling down curses from heaven: "Blow winds, and crack your cheeks! Rage, blow! … Crack nature's mold, all germens spill at once That makes ingrateful man" (*King Lear* 3.2.1, 9-11). The cursing is the same, as is the provocation, but the target has changed now: it is not Goneril and Regan, but the whole universe: "You cataracts and hurricanoes, spout Till you have drenched our steeples, drowned the cocks" (*King Lear* 3.2.2-4). If Lear's power had degenerated into impotent, inarticulate, empty threats in Act 2, scene 4, here he emerges in the storm with at least his verbal powers enhanced beyond anything he had had before; and since what he is shouting about is exactly what is taking place all around him, his words appear to us to be powerfully efficacious. Though the synopses may say Lear is raging against the elements, it may be more accurate to say he is raging *with* them against an unjust human world: all the staging (winds, rain, thunder, and lightning) is engaged in pathetic fallacy, with what Lear is feeling. And in his first speech here, Lear even appears to include himself among the targets to be obliterated by an angry or just heaven at his bidding: "You sulph'rous and thought-executing fires, Vaunt-couriers of oak-cleaving thunderbolts, Singe my white head" (*King Lear* 3.2.5-7). Here minus his misogyny, Lear's "perpetual outrage" is appealing and compelling because it is so universally human.[36]

---

[36] Thus Bloom, *Invention of the Human*, 510: "Perpetually outraged, except for the brief idyll of his reconciliation with Cordelia, Lear appeals primordially to the universal outrage of all those acutely conscious of their own mortality."

But in the following speeches, more of Lear's old self, old way of looking at and pitying his situation, creeps back into his description. He distinguishes the storm from his daughters (*King Lear* 3.2.17–21) but then accuses and blames the heavens for doing his daughters' bidding (*King Lear* 3.2.23–6). Then after a brief exchange with Kent and the Fool, in which Lear momentarily reasserts "patience" as the right response to this ordeal, he again shifts his perspective and interpretation of the storm, to an invocation of it as just retribution: "Let the great gods That keep this dreadful pudder o'er our heads Find out their enemies now" (*King Lear* 3.2.52–4). There follow several lines listing "undivulged crimes" (*King Lear* 3.2.55–62),[37] that will now finally be punished. One could imagine the next line would either veer back to a horrible description of either what Goneril and Regan did, or to the supposed retaliation about to be meted out on them. Lear could even, more hopefully and helpfully, list himself among such hidden criminals, one of the "simular[s] of virtue" (*King Lear* 3.2.57), who has now been exposed (literally) and chastened. But for now, Lear simply reverts to his usual self-pity: "I am a man More sinned against than sinning" (*King Lear* 3.2.62–3)—a line often, unfortunately used to summarize the attitude of the play overall.

But although Lear cannot accept responsibility, and is still pretty fixated on the unfairness of his own suffering, that suffering does begin to turn him toward considering and being compassionate toward the suffering of others: "My wits begin to turn. – Come on, my boy. How dost, my boy? Art cold? I am cold myself" (*King Lear* 3.2.73–5). Before, when Lear lamented his going mad (at *King Lear* 2.4.327), he feared the unmanly loss of control that would erupt in womanly tears, or (to counter that and stamp down such unwelcome outbursts) he threatened what seemed to him the more manly reaction of unspecified violence. But here, at the simple (and at least partly true) statement that he is being abused and disrespected, there is no eruption (and cleverly, the storm itself hides any tears he may be shedding), there is no outburst, but just a very gentle inquiry as to another's well-being, and a compassionate connection to someone suffering in the same way as he (he identifies with the Fool on their shared experience of being cold, even though Lear probably feels more acutely other pains that are not shared with the Fool or others).[38] I confess, as much as I love the play, the suddenness

---

[37]See Gil, *Shakespeare's Anti-Politics*, 108–209, on the incestuous imagery here and in Lear's cursing of Goneril in 1.4.
[38]Cf. Wasserman, "And Every One Have Need of Other," 23: "Only in this condition can Lear experience his bond with other men in its broadest, most essential form … In ethical terms

of this transformation in Lear is jarring and hard to accept, even by the standards of dramaturgy, that often require telescoping the passage of time or condensing events. One might have hoped for a few more lines or scenes to unfold the evolution more gradually. (As, indeed, the disrespect done to Lear by Goneril and Regan evolves and increases across a couple of scenes in Acts 1 and 2.) But perhaps the comparison with Augustine's "conversion" would be apt and helpful here. In Augustine's telling (which includes a lot of inner thoughts and silent prayers which are invisible and unknown to the audience of a stage play), all the preparation in the world can't really properly set the stage for us, the audience, or him, the subject, to understand or anticipate what happens in the garden in Book 8: it "just" happens, and generations of scholars and students have belabored it, wondering why it happens at that particular moment and not another, or if indeed it happened at all. A really life-changing transformation or conversion in a character (whether fictitious or historical) has to express continuity with both the previous self and the future self, for the conversion to be believable *and* eventful—even as we focus on the change or discontinuity in the subject's belief and behavior.[39] So here, the continuity with Lear's tendency to focus on himself and lament his own pain, is believable and convincing;[40] the further inclusion here of compassionate commiseration with another sufferer is sudden and novel for Lear, but a small addition, and also can be seen as a continuation of Lear's passionate, generous, at times overwrought

---

this occurs when he commits his first absolutely selfless act, urging the Fool to enter the hovel before him."

[39] The classic work, Arthur Darby Nock, *Conversion: The Old and the New in Religion from Alexander the Great to Augustine of Hippo* (Oxford: Oxford University Press, 1933), 7–8, puts more emphasis on the discontinuity, but acknowledges both elements:

> By conversion we mean the reorientation of the soul of an individual, his deliberate turning from indifference or from an earlier form of piety to another, a turning which implies a consciousness that a great change is involved, that the old was wrong and the new is right ... even when the fact of conversion appears wholly sudden and not led up to by a gradual process of gaining conviction, even when the convert may in all good faith profess that the beliefs which have won his sudden assent are new to him, there is a background of concepts to which a stimulus can give life.

[40] Recent studies, moreover, offer a more balanced representation, with more awareness of and emphasis on the continuity in the convert's life: see, for example, Daniel Winchester, "Converting to Continuity: Temporality and Self in Eastern Orthodox Conversion Narratives," *Journal for the Scientific Study of Religion* 54.3 (2015): 439–60, esp. 439: "Significantly, this rhetorical focus on continuity contrasts markedly with the majority of contemporary research on Christian conversion, which highlights narratives that emphasize an experience of temporal rupture or a 'complete break with the past.'"

personality.[41] This transformation leads to further realizations, first to an appreciation of things around him that Lear would have overlooked or despised before: "The art of our necessities is strange And can make vile things precious" (*King Lear* 3.2.76–7). I think I always misremember the line as "make vile things *seem* precious," but the claim in the original is stronger, more certain: the situation inflicted on us does not just trick us or temporarily alter our perception (like the heat reflected off a roadway deceives us into thinking there's water there)—it changes our reality because the change is in our values (what we deem precious), not just in our physical sense perception. And the impact of such necessities is heightened when they are painful. I certainly remember meals I have had with loved ones, and the experience is heightened and made more lasting by the good emotions being remembered in tandem with the sensory experience, but I don't think anything compares to the complete and radical transformation of a plastic bowl of green Jello into the most precious thing I've ever tasted because I ate it after being forced in the hospital, while in great pain, to add to my misery by not eating anything for several days. And curiously, the experience only works in one direction: a bad experience is not improved by association with a good experience, only by comparison with a worse one. Thus, I sometimes tease that I do not remember the best tiramisu I ever ate, but I can vividly recall the worst because I ate it at the most beautiful restaurant I was ever at (on the Grand Canal in Venice)—the disconnect between the beautiful setting and putting something akin to booze-soaked sheet cake into my mouth didn't improve the awful taste sensation; the memory was made more indelible, but not more pleasant.

And although the hovel is clearly one of the vile things that are now precious to Lear (*King Lear* 3.2.78), his focus is now not limited to it but expands to value his companions: "Poor Fool and knave, I have one part in my heart That's sorry yet for thee" (*King Lear* 3.2.79–80). Lear at this point doesn't mention his own suffering (as he did just above with the cold), but he has moved on to focus just on the Fool's discomfort and alleviating it.

The following scene has Lear return to his focus on himself and his own suffering (*King Lear* 3.4.17–25), but Kent's interruption and reminder of the hovel bring Lear back to the suffering of others:

---

[41] Bloom, *Invention of the Human*, 508, notes he "seems incapable of repressing anything whatsoever," and labels him with the sort of all inclusive quality of "wholeheartedness" (*Invention of the Human*, 509).

> Prithee, go in thyself. Seek thine own ease.
> This tempest will not give me leave to ponder
> On things would hurt me more. But I'll go in. --
> In, boy; go first. -- You houseless poverty --
> Nay, get thee in. I'll pray and then I'll sleep.
>
> (*King Lear* 3.4.27–31)

The similarity and even connectedness of the Fool's physical suffering to Lear's physical suffering has taken Lear away from focusing on his own mental anguish. Now it has expanded to include Kent as well, and also elicits from Lear a prayer, a prominent feature of Augustine's story in *Confessions*.[42] But what a prayer it is—not to God, but to all the destitute of the kingdom, among whom Lear now finds himself:

> Poor naked wretches wheresoe'er you are,
> That bide the pelting of this pitiless storm,
> How shall your houseless heads and unfed sides,
> Your looped and windowed raggedness defend you
> From seasons such as these?
>
> (*King Lear* 3.4.32–7)

As we will conclude, the play's lack of God or an afterlife makes a difference finally in interpreting the kind of humility Lear learns here, but for now note that humility—learning the value of others and prioritizing it above one's own well-being—is the central point and goal of this prayer, regardless of its addressee. And what we regretted as missing in Lear's earlier formulations here emerges—his taking painful responsibility for the general calamity all around him:

> O, I have ta'en
> Too little care of this. Take physic, pomp.
> Expose thyself to feel what wretches feel,
> That thou may'st shake the superflux to them
> And show the heavens more just.
>
> (*King Lear* 3.4.37–41)

---

[42] See Dunnington, "Humility," and Gladwin, "Embodying Humility," cited above.

Augustine's Confessions and Shakespeare's King Lear

This is an oddly beautiful image of universal and cosmic justice without a God, in which justice rises from the bottom up, not the top down. God does not impose or demand justice or punish its opposite, but Lear feels such kinship with his companions and even strangers, that he longs to be just towards them and thereby establish and increase justice.[43] This is the very opposite of Lear in the opening scene, exercising arbitrary power and calling it "just" because it emanates from him: now he humbly submits to others and gives them the necessities they lack, the very definition of compassion and equity, and therefore justice.[44]

But this is still to conceive of suffering humanity as somehow "out there," an object on to which non-suffering humanity (those with a surplus), can bestow benefits and to which they can give attention. But Lear no longer has any surplus—no power to exercise on behalf of the destitute. He himself is wretched and powerless; he can only "feel what wretches feel." Lear is on the verge of identifying with the powerless when Edgar then appears, disguised as a "poor naked wretch." Identifying with Edgar at first runs in the opposite direction for Lear—not taking on himself the other's suffering, but absorbing Edgar into Lear's continuing fantasy of his own persecution: "Didst thou give all to thy daughters? And art thou come to this?" (*King Lear* 3.4.53–4). It's not compassion if one simply projects one's own feelings onto a fellow sufferer and then feels sorry for them (and thereby, sorry for oneself). That would just be a melodramatic version of self-pity and only appear other-directed when it's not. But Edgar's acting does move Lear slightly away from self-pity and to a deeper feeling of connection with him: "Thou wert better in a grave than to answer with thy uncovered body this extremity of the skies. -- Is man no more than this? ... Thou art the thing itself; unaccommodated man is no more but such a poor, bare, forked animal as thou art" (*King Lear* 3.4.108–10, 113–14). The "cheap as beasts" life Lear had spurned in his final confrontation with Regan, he now embraces and aligns himself with, by disrobing to be more like the mostly naked Edgar and identify with him.[45] Such fellow-feeling even expands to be outright respect

---

[43] The dynamic is similar in Act 3, scene 7, when the servants defend and help Gloucester, and conclude their efforts with, "Now heaven help him!" (*King Lear* 3.7.129).

[44] It may, however, not be possible in the world of the play. See Greenblatt, *Shakespeare's Freedom*, 92: "At the height of the storm scene, the crazed Lear, exposed to the tyranny of the elements, has a fleeting glimpse of a relationship to power different from the one he had embodied ... but nothing in the play suggests it is remotely possible to achieve."

[45] Cf. Schulman, *Rethinking Shakespeare's Political Philosophy*, 115: "Sovereignty's inheritor must be radically depersonalised for authority to be adequately reconstructed. Lear's famous dirge on

and admiration for Edgar, as Lear calls him a "philosopher" (*King Lear* 3.4.162, 189), "learned Theban" (*King Lear* 3.4.165), "noble philosopher" (*King Lear* 3.4.183), and "good Athenian" (*King Lear* 3.4.193).

The painful interplay between compassion and self-pity continues in the trial scene (Act 3, scene 6). Lear in his madness enacts a deranged version of the opening scene,[46] passing judgment and assigning punishment to Goneril and Regan, and specifying the kind of horrible violence he had fantasized in Act 2, scene 4, but had been unable to even put it into words while still sane: "To have a thousand with red burning spits Come hissing in upon 'em!" (*King Lear* 3.6.15–16). But with Edgar and the Fool, Lear's kindness and consideration continues, calling them, "learned justice" (*King Lear* 3.6.21-2), and "sapient sir" (*King Lear* 3.6.23). And when Lear reappears in Act 4, scene 6, he incredibly claims, "I am the king himself ... Ay, every inch a king" (*King Lear* 4.6.103, 127). But alongside this assertion of royalty gained by seeing his common humanity, there is again the slippage back into asserting power over others and self-pity that such power is not obeyed—a claimed strength that is as fragile and needy as it was in the original opening scene: "When I do stare, see how the subject quakes ... Gloucester's bastard son was kinder to his father than my daughters got 'tween lawful sheets" (*King Lear* 4.6.133-4). Such assertions of "power" are anything but, degenerating into hysterical, misogynistic fantasies of cuckoldry or castration: "Down from the waist they are centaurs, though women all above. But to the girdle do the gods inherit; beneath is all the fiend's. There's hell, there's darkness, there's the sulphurous pit; burning, scalding, stench, consumption!" (*King Lear* 4.6.140-4).[47] (Again—more on this in a subsequent chapter.)

But Lear's sense of real strength through weakness, transparency, and submission, continues to grow as he considers the blinded Gloucester and himself. He refuses Gloucester's offer of obeisance, because they are in the same condition: "O, let me kiss that hand! / Let me wipe it first; it

---

'unaccomodated man' is not just mused generally, but provoked literally by the sight of Edgar." Also Wasserman, "And Every One Have Need of Other," 23: "Only in this condition can Lear experience his bond with other men in its broadest, most essential form. On the heath amid the storm, ... all the narrow bounds of role and position dissolve."

[46]Cf. Wasserman, "And Every One Have Need of Other," 24: "But he is only a travesty of the king who dominated the first scene; and this entire scene is a kind of ironic reprise of the original ... Lear conceives of his relationship with his subjects in terms of his absolute authority ... he is only a grotesque and pathetic burlesque of a king."

[47]Schulman, *Rethinking Shakespeare's Political Philosophy*, 110, labels these lines as "Lear's naturalistic deracination reaches its apogee, in febrile misogyny."

smells of mortality" (*King Lear* 4.6.147-8). Lear then goes into a litany of how conventional (human but also masculine) attempts at "justice" are just force and violence masquerading as such, culminating with the example, "Thou hast seen a farmer's dog bark at a beggar? ... And the creature run from the cur? There thou might'st behold the great image of authority: a dog's obeyed in office" (*King Lear* 4.6.169-70, 172-4). And Lear repeats his gesture of disrobing to remove any vestiges of society or royalty, and attain the simplicity, innocence, and purity that he earlier saw in Edgar and now tries to uncover in himself (*King Lear* 4.6.191).[48] Edgar underlines for us, the audience, how perceptive or transformative all this is, by saying, "O, matter and impertinency mixed, Reason in madness!" (*King Lear* 4.6.193-4). Lear's then identifying with Gloucester is not by projecting his specific woes onto him (as previously), but a much more general compassion for shared misery and an eager connection to alleviate it: "If thou wilt weep my fortunes, take my eyes. I know thee well enough; thy name is Gloucester. Thou must be patient. We came crying hither; Thou knowest the first time that we smell the air We wawl and cry" (*King Lear* 4.6.194-8). Paradoxically, this leads to Lear's first assertion of violence against his sons-in-law, rather than the misogynistic fantasies he indulged in up until now (*King Lear* 4.6.204-5). An ordeal can be humbly and patiently borne only if its source is truthfully acknowledged.

This mutual suffering and compassion continue and intensify in the two scenes of reunion with Cordelia (Act 4, scene 7; Act 5, scene 3), accompanied by mutual signs of submission.[49] Cordelia asks her father's blessing, and after Lear apparently attempts to kneel before her, she forbids it (*King Lear* 4.7.166-7). Lear can acknowledge the evils done to him by Goneril and Regan, without expressions of rage or revenge, but instead leading to his own admission of wrongdoing (*King Lear* 4.7.81-5). Both Lear and Cordelia

---

[48] Cf. Schulman, *Rethinking Shakespeare's Political Philosophy*, 108: "He [Lear] is flummoxed by the political transition he inadvertently set in motion. Social identity determined by location in a fixed hierarchy gives way to universally shared status based on a new naturalism."

[49] Cf. Wasserman, "And Every One Have Need of Other," 24:

> Significantly, Lear loses this sense of himself as king with the passing of his madness. He confronts Cordelia ... with the same great dignity he attained on the heath. And his expression of his relationship to Cordelia epitomizes the essential meaning of 'bond' that he discovered there ... He is a man and she a lady, they are human beings—that is their primary relationship. She is *also* his child.
>
> (emphasis in original)

acknowledge their parent-child bond (*King Lear* 4.7.79-80), but Lear makes the only demand appropriate for such a relationship—understanding: "You must bear with me. Pray you now, forget, and forgive. I am old and foolish" (*King Lear* 4.7.97-9). The last we see of them both alive, Lear describes a tragically beautiful future of such reciprocal respect and affection: "When thou dost ask me blessing, I'll kneel down and ask of thee forgiveness" (*King Lear* 5.3.11-12). Significantly, the life Lear fantasizes is distanced from power, but still can witness the painful, ever-changing exercise of such, at a safe distance:[50]

> So we'll live,
> And pray, and sing, and tell old tales, and laugh
> At gilded butterflies, and hear poor rogues
> Talk of court news, and we'll talk with them too --
> Who loses and who wins; who's in, and who's out,
> And take upon 's the mystery of things,
> As if we were God's spies. And we'll wear out,
> In a walled prison, packs and sects of great ones
> That ebb and flow by th' moon.
>
> (*King Lear* 5.3.12-20)

No longer desiring to be a "great one," wielding arbitrary power, Lear longs for the unchanging constancy and peace of humility and mutual submission.

In a way, Goneril's penultimate line, "[T]he laws are mine, not thine. Who can arraign me for 't?" (*King Lear* 5.3.189-90), provides the final word on Lear's behavior in the opening scene, and on all those (Goneril, Regan, Edmund, Cornwall), who have tried to seize such arbitrary power for themselves.[51] Lear was his own law, as Goneril nearly is at the end—answerable to no one, doing whatever s/he feels like, and judged only by the results (which are complete destruction for both, as well as most of the rest of the cast). What the play spends so much time developing in Acts 3 and 4, is Lear's experience of humility and connectedness with other people—an

---

[50] The insight of Schulman, *Rethinking Shakespeare's Political Philosophy*, 122: "Yet this final location of love's unfolding, the prison where he can finally 'unburthened crawl toward death' (I, i, 39), is not exactly free of power. Lear's private realm seems to *depend* for its value on comparison with an inconstant public world."

[51] Cf. Davis, "My Master Calls Me," 59: "For Goneril and Regan, as well as other characters in the play, political authority is conceptualized as something defeasible—something that does not persistently adhere in a person but can be transferred from one person to another."

alternative to the arbitrary power he exercised at the beginning and which Goneril or Regan would have continued if they could have.

In both our texts, *King Lear* and *Confessions*, the protagonist had valued himself over others (and most especially and frequently over women)—seen himself as smarter, more powerful, more valuable; in both, they achieve a right understanding of their mistake and of their real position, realizing they are not above others. The two texts we are considering begin and end similarly on this point—but for very different reasons, and with very different ultimate conclusions. For Augustine, the corrective to pride is seeing how far above himself God is, and God has shown his superiority not just to Augustine and all humans, but even to the sinfulness and death that separates God from all of His creation: God has conquered death by being willing to die, whereas we just have to die, and thereby show our complete defeat by death without God. Humility, then, for Augustine has to include hope (or even assurance) of a resurrection and a future with God—because God's greatness, by which He humbles us, includes the ability to conquer death, by which he will exalt us.[52] But for Lear, humility on the heath and at the end, is a realization of the previously devalued (or at least unappreciated) value of other human beings—God is not part of this realization.[53] Lear exalts others to humble himself, and in the end shows a kinship, and love for them that he seemed incapable (or at least unaware) of at the beginning, when he exalted himself and disregarded their value or connection to himself. And paradoxically, it may not even just be kinship, it may even be a return and reconstitution of his *king*ship: through his humiliation/humility, Lear achieves a "sovereign nothingness" that is like the kenotic power of Christ (without it having salvific effects, or any effects for anyone other than himself), and is real power, unlike the false assertion of vain and arbitrary power with which the play began.[54]

But the differences in the final conclusions of the two texts, on humility and power, can be stated quite starkly. Augustine learns to love God more

---

[52] Cf. Ruddy, "Humble God," 88: "It was inconceivable to him that humility could be valued apart from a belief in the Incarnation."

[53] Cf. Schulman, *Rethinking Shakespeare's Political Philosophy*, 106, 116: "But *Lear* makes better sense as a non-theological (re)creation of human beings: a secularised Genesis tracing the birth of a modern regime, a theoretically egalitarian realm of contract and consent … Lear's Act 5 misinterpretation of regaining consciousness as having been brought back from the dead indicates transition, not from Paganism to Christianity, but from religious enchantment to materialism."

[54] "Sovereign nothingness" is from Sheerin, "Making Use of Nothing," 808, who concludes by explicating it in political terms:

than any human, including himself; Lear learns to love others more than himself.[55] Both are huge realizations that sick, sinful ego usually stands in the way of, for normal people such as ourselves. But both are quite capable of dehumanizing extremes, if in opposite ways. For Lear (the character or the play) can be consumed by hopelessness, despair, or nihilism, that others, even if he loves them more than himself, are still and only just meat puppets who are going to die soon along with him.[56] One needn't dwell on the love and beauty he has found briefly and at great cost, which his pride previously kept from him; one can turn from it (as the audience is forced to), to consider only what is also included in what Lear now sees clearly—namely death, misery, malice, torture, and cruelty—that his pride and the delusions of power and convention had also kept from him previously, an "image of that horror" (*King Lear* 5.3.317). For Augustine, loving only God to the exclusion of everything and everyone else, may slip toward carelessness toward other humans and their suffering; if my own suffering doesn't bother me, because I have complete faith that God can heal it, then the suffering of others shouldn't bother me either because God can be relied on to heal them, too. Lear's humility is a kind of compassionate hopelessness: "Buck up, fellow sufferer; death is the ultimate cure for your suffering. And we all will experience that soon enough."[57] Augustine's may seem too much like hopeful, even dismissive apathy: "Thoughts and prayers. Don't worry; be happy. God will make things right in the end." Neither alone seems like the

---

The scene on the heath is undoubtedly a low point from a materialist and even existentialist perspective, but politically it marks the birth of something profoundly promising – here Lear (even unbeknownst to him) is able to rally his subjects and spur them on to service on behalf of the state, to challenging those who threaten it … Lear suddenly begins to acquire again what he had lost, now without even a trace of effort,
("Making Use of Nothing," 810)

See also Greenblatt, *Shakespeare's Freedom*, 93: "He had begun with a king who wished to withdraw from power and reassure himself with comfortable falsehoods, public affirmations of his own limitless importance and generosity that he demanded of his children. In the course of the play those falsehoods are relentlessly stripped away, like the train of followers who had given the imperious Lear a sense of his own worth."

[55] Cf. Schulman, *Rethinking Shakespeare's Political Philosophy*, 116, referring to Edgar: "Human action replaces divine intervention."

[56] Thus Bloom, *Invention of the Human*, 506: "You can deny the pragmatic nihilism of *King Lear* or *Hamlet* if you are a firm enough theist, but you will be rather beside the point, for Shakespeare neither challenges nor endorses your hopes for a personal resurrection."

[57] Though I am struck by how even the persistence of hope in a grim, uncertain world, can be taken as further confirmation that one should continue in such hope, as Tishman, "Review," 429–30, movingly writes: "I like Lear's world better than Augustine's, to be honest … I have

kind of deep, passionate devotion to others to alleviate their suffering and help bring them together with us to long term (or perhaps even eternal, if that is possible) joy and fulfillment, which I think all people of any religious commitment (or none at all) are striving for in their various ways. On this point, I think our two texts do not so much individually reveal partial truths, as they reveal incompatible, unacceptable extremes that we as readers or audience try to hold or moderate together.

---

spent the last five years working as a hospital chaplain. I left academia just in time for a global pandemic. Nearly every day I confront the wonder of human meaning-making in the face of a world with no assurances." It is also a devotion to truth. See Greenblatt, *Shakespeare's Freedom*, 94: "But the terrible sense of limit articulated at the close – the weight, the sadness of the time, the need to obey – has brought with it the strange injunction that is one of Shakespeare's most remarkable gifts, the simple injunction to speak what we feel."

CHAPTER 3
AUGUSTINE AND WOMEN IN *CONFESSIONS*

In discussing women in *Confessions*, we must first specify how and what we are attempting in our analysis because the topic can be developed in several ways. We could try to construct a general theory about women that Augustine developed in *Confessions* (and elsewhere).[1] Equally ambitious but a very different project would be to piece together the historical realities behind the text—the real people on which the narrative is based, the facts of whose lives are now partly revealed but also partly obscured and altered by the story Augustine tells.[2] The first would be theoretical (anthropological or sociological), the latter historical. My analysis here is much more modest and purely literary: how does Augustine *depict* the women in his telling of *Confessions*—regardless of how they were in real life, and without generalizing these depictions to other women. To specify

---

[1] Cf. the programmatic statement near the beginning of Kate Cooper, *Queens of a Fallen World: The Lost Women of Augustine's Confessions* (London: Basic Books, 2023), 3: "But with Monnica of Thagaste, this changes. Alone among the women of the ancient Mediterranean world, Monnica raised a son who not only noticed women but explored in depth what he learned from them and broadcast what he learned to the wider world." Nearer the end of this book, Cooper also shows this attitude benefited Augustine as an author:

> In his years as a bishop, Augustine would discover a gift for friendship with women, corresponding with a network of influential heiresses from powerful Christian families across the empire, especially in the Italian circles surrounding the court and the Senate. These women played an important role in carrying his writings to a wider readership and ultimately in ensuring the preservation of his legacy after this death.
>
> (*Queens of a Fallen World*, 218)

[2] This is the project overall for Cooper, *Queens of a Fallen World*; for such a reconstruction for Monica specifically, see also Gillian Clark, *Monica: An Ordinary Saint* (Oxford: Oxford University Press, 2015). Similarly, for a historical reconstruction of the concubine, see Margaret R. Miles, "Not Nameless but Unnamed: The Woman Torn from Augustine's Side," in *Feminist Interpretations of Augustine*, edited by Judith Chelius Stark (University Park: Pennsylvania State University Press, 2007), 167–88.

how *Confessions* presents more challenges than *King Lear* (or any work of fiction): throughout we are completely reliant on Augustine's thoughts of and attitudes toward these women, not the thoughts, words, and actions of the women themselves.[3] Of course that is also true of Shakespeare, but since Augustine is both author and character in his own story, the situation is more complex—as though we got information about some characters only from the point of view of another character and not from an omniscient narrator who was equally responsible for creating all the characters. (And drama is further limited in a different way from narrative fiction, in that we don't know the thoughts of any of the characters on stage.)

Even confining our analysis to literary concerns can go in several directions. Too often, the urge seems to be to trace the ways in which a character is a symbol—and only a symbol—and leave it at that. I'm thinking especially of the scenario similar to Augustine's, with how analysis is done of Beatrice (a character in a work of fiction who is based on a real woman the author knew) from Dante's *Commedia*. The analysis, then, is like cracking a code: once the reality hidden behind the character is found, the puzzle is solved and finished. In the case of interpreting allegorical texts, this is surely the main goal in interpretation, and a text remains obscure or meaningless until its elements are decoded. But neither *King Lear* nor *Confessions* (especially the autobiographical Books 1–9) is best read (or only read) as an allegory. Both have plots and develop characters, and these should be analyzed primarily for their meaning within the text, as opposed to bringing in some outside referent to explain them. This does not eliminate echoes or influences from other texts and traditions but considers such factors as secondary to the primary text we are considering and interpreting. Thus, many such influences on the primary text should be acknowledged in passing, or as we go, without it being the final word of analysis.

---

[3] This is noted for both Monica and the concubine. For Monica, cf. Kitty Bouwman, "Spiritual Motherhood of Monnica: Two Mothers in the Life of Saint Augustine," *Studies in Spirituality* 29 (2019): 49–69, esp. 51: "An important reservation must be noted in advance, namely that for this presentation, we are totally dependent on the way in which Augustine presented her spiritual motherhood. Everything we know about Monnica is written from his perspective." On the concubine, cf. Miles, "Not Nameless," 168: "Augustine's partner creates for a feminist historian some interesting historiographical questions. Most historians' interest in this 'nameless woman' is limited to understanding her in order to understand Augustine better. Is there enough evidence of her to permit us to reconstruct *her* historical presence? My answer will be yes and no" (emphasis in original).

Augustine and Women in *Confessions*

There are two women in *Confessions* who will be the main focus of our attention and analysis in this chapter—Augustine's mother, Monica; and the unnamed woman with whom he lived for many years and who bore him a son, in most commentaries still labeled "the concubine."[4] Monica (and Augustine's whole story) is meant to evoke the story of the Prodigal Son (Luke 15:11–32), as Augustine explicitly states (*Conf.* 2.10.18).[5] Also frequently observed is how Monica is meant to remind us throughout of our mother, the Church.[6] More obscurely but still interesting is the possible influence from Manichean depictions of the "Mother of Life," to which Monica in *Confessions* would be a contrast or anti-type.[7] Going in the other direction, of how her depiction in *Confessions* shaped later traditions, Boethius's Lady Philosophy seems modeled on Monica here.[8] Taking individual elements of these influences and considering how they interact to create the overall depiction of Monica, as well as considering non-typical elements, rather than focusing on one influence as the determinative, guiding principle, will be our interpretive challenge.

To start with Monica: it seems the most obvious analysis of her in *Confessions* includes two main elements—first, that she displays behavior and attitudes typical of mothers. She is maternal throughout; her other identities or roles (e.g. wife, daughter, believer) are only glimpsed briefly before the focus is again fixed on her as a mother. And even given the vast separation in time from the fourth century to now, many of these characteristics are familiar to us as we consider mothers in our own time and find similarities to those of the fourth century—for example, nurturing, protection, and security. And secondly, these maternal characteristics are selectively highlighted by the

---

[4]Cf. Cooper, *Queens of a Fallen World*, who treats both of them at length, but adds Justina, empress of Rome (mentioned at *Conf.* 9.7.15), and the girl to whom Augustine was engaged (mentioned at *Conf.* 6.13.23). Also cf. Miles, "Not Nameless but Unnamed," 168: "Let us begin by recognizing that Augustine's partner was not 'nameless'. Rather, Augustine did not reveal her name."

[5]Cf. Marianne Djiuth, "Augustine, Monica, and the Love of Wisdom," *Augustinian Studies* 39.2 (2008): 237–52, esp. 230–1; Johannes Van Oort, "Monnica's Bishop and the 'filius istarum lacrimarum' (*Conf.* 3,21)," *Church History and Religious Culture* 103 (2023): 1–21, esp. 18.

[6]Cf. John Sehorn, "Monica as Synecdoche for the Pilgrim Church in the *Confessiones*," 46.2 (2015): 225–48; with some further nuance, Douglas Finn, "The Holy Spirit and the Church in the Earliest Augustine: An Analysis of the Character of Monnica in the Cassiciacum Dialogues," *Papers Presented at the Seventeenth International Conference on Patristic Studies* 24 (2017): 141–65.

[7]Thus Van Oort, "Monnica's Bishop and the 'filius istarum lacrimarum' (*Conf.* 3,21)," esp. 18–21.

[8]Richard Upsher Smith, "Saint Monica and Lady Philosophy," *Carmina Philosophiae* 18 (2009): 93–125.

author Augustine primarily to contrast with himself: Monica's care, piety, and patience are all set in opposition to Augustine's careless, irresponsible behavior; his faithless, anxious seeking; and his restless, irascible nature.[9] In episode after episode, the implicit or explicit contrast to Augustine's sinful behavior is that the reader cannot imagine Monica ever having done such things (e.g., theft, ostentatious weeping at the theater, changing fundamental beliefs or philosophies several times, living with someone to whom she is not married). Perhaps most succinctly, it is all contained in the role of "mother" not being reciprocal, as partner or sibling should be: as his mother, Monica is throughout focused on Augustine's success,[10] but as a child, even an adult child, he is not focused on her needs. One could note that they are in agreement, both working toward the same goal, in that both are focused on Augustine's well-being, but part of the deeper irony of Augustine's analysis is that ultimately the things he does against his mother's wishes do not make him happier or more fulfilled, any more than anything else he does. Until his "conversion," much of Augustine's journey could be summarized as, "Once again, as usual, I should have listened to my mother."

The straightforward and repeated contrast of the pious, obedient Monica with the sinful, wayward Augustine certainly makes sense of most of his story in *Confessions*. "Monica—good, Augustine—bad" is accurate and goes a long way to describing the obstacles and suspense of the narrative. How long can Augustine be willful and self-destructive, in the face of such steadfast and divinely approved love? It is the kind of reading one would welcome and encourage in a first-time reader, and which one still feels oneself drawn to, even after repeated study. How much of world literature can be summarized as "true love conquers all"—perhaps more often romantic love, but here a mother's love for an undeserving child who finally comes

---

[9] Cf. Marianne Djuth, "Augustine, Monica, and the Love of Wisdom," *Augustinian Studies* 39.2 (2008): 231–2, esp.228: "Augustine's insight in *Confessions* 9,4 into the disparity between the condition of his soul and Monica's at Cassiciacum has as its basis a series of contrasts or oppositions that he draws between Monica and himself throughout the first eight books of *Confessions*."

[10] Monica had other children—and Augustine had siblings—but she seems to have been focused on Augustine, at least in his telling: cf. Gillian Clark, *Monica: An Ordinary Saint* (Oxford: Oxford University Press, 2015): 31–2. Clarissa W. Atkinson, "'Your Servant, My Mother': The Figure of Saint Monica in the Ideology of Christian Motherhood," in *Immaculate & Powerful: The Female in Sacred Image and Social Reality*, edited by Clarissa W. Atkinson, Constance H. Buchanan, and Margaret R. Miles. The Harvard Women's Studies in Religion series (Boston: Beacon Press, 1985): 139–72, esp. 141, says Augustine "was her mission and her destiny."

to appreciate all the sacrifice that has been made on his behalf? Quoting a nineteenth-century scholar, a recent meditation on Monica shows the appeal and continued relevance of such an analysis: "Believing Monica had possessed 'the most beautiful love that ever existed', Bougaud encouraged mothers to look to her example and recognize 'how divine is the strength with which God has endowed them in the interest of their children's eternal salvation.'"[11] In the battle of wills, Monica will inevitably win, and we will rejoice when she does: "Bougaud goes on to explain that a mother's divine strength consists of her ability to bring about her children's salvation through her own steadfast will."[12]

All of this is true and accurate—but only up to a point, and only as a starting point: "But the physical bond of mother and child should not be overvalued."[13] There is even something opposite between parenting and the overall dynamic of *Confessions*: Augustine's narrative seeks to find the unity in life and existence, while parenting is necessarily about differentiation and separation.[14] And as for Monica's saintliness: even in the details of how Monica's story is told, it has been noted that Monica's life, while praised throughout by Augustine, is not exactly presented as a hagiography, a biography of a female saint, or a "woman-of-worth."[15] It is not idealized or exemplary, but more realistic, and its lessons are subtler than "go and do likewise" (just as Augustine's story is something more complex than "Don't live as I did.")[16] Being a righteous mother is contrasted with being a sinful child in *Confessions*, but it does not confer infallibility, perfection, or sinlessness. Rather, the qualities of a mother are repeated and focused in the

---

[11] Matthew Haste, "'So Many Voices': The Piety of Monica, Mother of Augustine," *The Journal of Family Ministry* 4 (2013): 6–10, quotation on p. 6.
[12] Ibid.
[13] Gillian Clark, *Monica: An Ordinary Saint* (Oxford: Oxford University Press, 2015): 164.
[14] Cf. Carnes, Natalie, Motherhood: A Confession (Stanford: Stanford University Press, 2020) 5: "Yet the central drama of parenthood is not of two wills becoming one; it is of one will becoming two, as the parent helps bring the child into fullness."
[15] See Clark, *Monica: An Ordinary Saint*, 157–258.
[16] Thus Rebecca Moore, "O Mother, Where Art Thou? In Search of Saint Monnica," in *Feminist Interpretations of Augustine*, edited by Judith Chelius Stark (University Park: Pennsylvania State University Press, 2007). 147–66, esp. 150–251:

> The characterization of Monnica as maternal and female may reveal traces of the woman herself because Augustine is using these categories to point out her weaknesses, her worldliness, her sinfulness ... I look at Monnica, therefore, at her ordinariness, her infinite banality, within the context of woman-of-worth narratives. She runs counter to the heroic type in many ways, and this places her in sharp relief.

Augustine's Confessions and Shakespeare's King Lear

person of Monica. Most often, these qualities are positive (and contrasted with the opposite qualities in Augustine). But to build outward from the end of the autobiographical part of the narrative: one may have noticed above that my characterization of Monica as seemingly incapable of theft seems accurate, when Augustine narrates his own theft in Book 2 but turns out not to be the whole story when he later reveals that as a child, Monica stole wine from her parents:

> In spite of this, something had stealthily snared your handmaiden – as she told me, her son – a furtive fondness for wine: whenever, in accord with custom, her parents sent this responsible daughter of theirs to draw wine from the cask by dipping a cup in through an opening near the head, she would take a tiny sip by touching it with her lips before pouring it into the decanter. Repugnance prevented her from taking more, for she was acting not from any real craving for drink, but from a certain exuberance of youthful naughtiness, which is apt to erupt in playful behavior, and is usually curbed when it appears in children by the authority of their elders. But by adding to that modest allowance daily modest allowances – for one who allows himself license in little things is ruined little by little – she had fallen at length into the habit of avidly quaffing near goblets-full of wine.[17]

At the very end of her story and life, while in his way eulogizing his mother for her many virtues, Augustine works in a story of her sinfulness. That seemingly incongruous episode should make us reevaluate the entire depiction of Monica and make us more alert to hints of sinful behavior by her throughout. (Again—even if Augustine's outward, overt, more extravagantly sinful behavior is foregrounded throughout and meant as the main focus of our analysis, contrast, and disapproval.)

So Monica's maternal instincts and behavior, while mostly virtuous and in stark and repeated contrast with Augustine's sinful life, also contain traces of sinfulness (as much as Augustine wants to excuse it—"a certain exuberance of youthful naughtiness"). Her maternal character is not equivalent to God's judgment and sometimes leads the person following it to behave badly. The almost primal, instinctive manifestation of such maternal love is the overwhelming desire for the child's physical presence—that he be near his

---

[17] *Conf.* 9.8.18.

mother, able to be seen, heard, touched. This is vividly depicted at the end of Book 5, as Augustine describes his sneaking off to Rome and leaving his mother behind, weeping and wailing:

> So the wind blew for us and filled our sails, and the shore dropped away from our sight as she stood there at morning light mad with grief, filling your ears with complaints and groans. You took no heed, for you were snatching me away, using my lusts to put an end to them and chastising her too-carnal desire with the scourge of sorrow. Like all mothers, though far more than most, she loved to have me with her, and she did not know how much joy you were to create for her through my absence. She did not know, and so she wept and wailed, and these cries of pain revealed what there was left of Eve in her, as in anguish she sought the son whom in anguish she had brought to birth. Yet when she had finished blaming my deception and cruelty, she resumed her entreaties for me, and returned to her accustomed haunts, while I went to Rome.[18]

Augustine is described as following his "lusts," but his mother is immersed in the "too-carnal desire" typical of mothers, and she is even compared to Eve.[19] Both Augustine and Monica are sinful and receive correction by God, who uses them for His own good ends (not the selfish and short-sighted ends of the sinful humans who feel and follow their own desires), which are what bring real "joy."

It may seem hyperbolic to the reader—especially given how vividly he describes the bubbling swamp of fleshly desires and the images with which he describes sin as starvation and festering sores—when Augustine earlier describes how loving a female partner becomes confused and degraded by lust:

---

[18]*Conf.* 5.8. 15.
[19]Cf. Carl Avren Levenson, "Distance and Presence in Augustine's 'Confessions,'" *The Journal of Religion* 65.4 (October 1985): 500–12, esp. 501–2,

> But though the infant in its need can receive the mother's generosity, the child will discover its oppressive and threatening aspect ... So here there is an excess of intimacy, of presence, and it makes the child uneasy. To be sure, the mother gives and *wants* only to give; but she tends, through her gifts, to reabsorb the child she has lost.
>
> (emphasis original)

> So I arrived at Carthage, where the din of scandalous love-affairs raged cauldron-like around me. I was not yet in love, but I was enamored with the idea of love, and so deep within me was my need that I hated myself for the sluggishness of my desires. In love with loving, I was casting about for something to love; the security of a way of life free from pitfalls seemed abhorrent to me, because I was inwardly starved of that food which is yourself, O my God. Yet this inner famine created no pangs of hunger in me. I had no desire for the food that does not perish, not because I had my fill of it, but because the more empty I was, the more I turned from it in revulsion. My soul's health was consequently poor. It was covered with sores and flung itself out of doors, longing to soothe its misery by rubbing against sensible things; yet these were soulless, and so could not be truly loved. Loving and being loved were sweet to me, the more so if I could enjoy a lover's body; so I polluted the stream of friendship with my filthy desires and clouded its purity with hellish lusts; yet all the while, befouled and disgraced though I was, my boundless vanity made me long to appear elegant and sophisticated. I blundered headlong into the love which I hoped would hold me captive, but in your goodness, O my God, my mercy, you sprinkled bitter gall over my sweet pursuits. I was loved, and I secretly entered into an enjoyable liaison, but I was also trammeling myself with fetters of distress, laying myself open to the iron rods and burning scourges of jealousy and suspicion, of fear, anger and quarrels.[20]

But as overblown as the description is, many of us do look with regret on the things we did as teenagers or young adults, perhaps even condemn them more vehemently than we need to, so perhaps Augustine's description here is not so hard to believe. But it is harder to see here how natural, maternal love can be sinful and "too-carnal." It is how he conceives of it, however. (And to be fair, and going beyond the examples in the text—one need only think of really dysfunctional parent–child relationships, to see that they can be very sinful and destructive indeed.) Whether it is romantic partners or parent/child, human relationships for Augustine are ultimately like everything else earthly: they now exist in a fallen, sinful state. They are therefore always liable to mislead us by mistaking or confusing a spiritual reality with how it

---

[20]*Conf.* 3.1.1.

is perceived in its physical manifestation; such relationships may even try to usurp the credit and praise due to God for His providence and care.[21]

This is perhaps the most obvious, physical expression of maternal care that can have a sinful, selfish aspect. But it can be much more deliberate, conscious, and non-physical—and Monica definitely is shown with such urges, too, perhaps more often and more pervasively than her weeping at Augustine's sinful departure. As we consider again, the "conversion" that Augustine undergoes in *Confessions*, we should focus on its having at least two parts or elements—a change in what he believes, and a change in his lifestyle and behavior. Either of these could have further distinctions or divisions within them, and how they relate is still confusing to those of us who have carefully read the account many times.[22] But what I am now referring to vaguely as "change in lifestyle" can deeply influence the worldly status, wealth, power, and prestige that Augustine will enjoy, going forward. In other words, he may well be changing his life to improve his material prospects (or at least, those may be improved, coincidentally, depending on how he changes his lifestyle).[23] All of us who are parents have said at some point, "It doesn't matter, as long as my children are happy," in reference to our children moving, changing jobs, beginning or ending relationships; but if we are honest, we all know that some changes look to us as more probably beneficial, and we rejoice at them (if we don't actively push or try to persuade our children to go in the direction or decision we prefer). And

---

[21] Cf. Carnes, *Motherhood*, 12, 24:

> I thought as a parent I would feel your infant presence as an extension of my own body – or at least as flesh and blood I myself had produced, shaped, and molded ... It is not my milk that holds you in being, gives you life, or saves you. I have confused the image with imaged – milk with love, myself with life-giver.

Carnes here perceptively and helpfully shows the further confusion (besides physical versus spiritual) of mistaking oneself for the source of life and goodness.

[22] Cf. Felix B. A. Asiedu, "Following the Example of a Woman: Augustine's Conversion to Christianity in 386," *Vigiliae Christianae* 57.3 (August 2003): 276–306; see esp. 284: "Bk. 7 gives a coherent and tidy account of the various errors from which he was converted, preparing the way for the climactic scene. The intellectual odyssey in Bk. 7, however, seems to have little bearing on the theme of sexual renunciation which concludes Bk. 8."

[23] Ibid., 276–7:

> Augustine also describes his mother's new joy, and relates for the first time that in Monnica's attempts for her son's marriage we must see not only her desire for his conversion but even the domestic joys of seeing Augustine's offspring ... The concern here for grandchildren falls into that general order of earthly desires which comes in for criticism in the early part of the *Confessions*.

Monica seems to have made her preferences clear, as regards Augustine's ending his relationship with Adeodatus' mother and becoming engaged to a more suitable (i.e., advantageous, wealthy) young woman.[24] Simply put, Monica shared and even encouraged Augustine's worldly ambitions; she seems just as committed to social climbing and upward mobility as he. (If anything, his description of his own, deep sorrow at casting off Adeodatus' mother would make it seem Monica was more committed and more callous to the costs of such social advancement—or at least Augustine perceives and depicts her as such.) And his "conversion" finally includes not just sexual renunciation but also quitting his prestigious, upwardly mobile job, and breaking off his engagement to a well born, wealthy girl who could also assist in this ascent up the social hierarchy—that is, the dashing of Monica's ambitions too, though with his description of Monica's joy at his conversion, he claims she too had abandoned such hopes and gladly accepted God's will:

> We went indoors and told my mother, who was overjoyed. When we related to her how it had happened she was filled with triumphant delight and blessed you, who have power to do more than we ask or understand, for she saw that you had granted her much more in my regard than she had been wont to beg of you in her wretched, tearful groaning. Many years earlier you had shown her a vision of me standing on the rule of faith, and now indeed I stood there, no longer seeking a wife or entertaining any worldly hope, for you had converted me to yourself. In so doing you had also converted her grief into a joy far more abundant than she had desired, and much more tender and chaste than she could ever have looked to find in grandchildren from my flesh.[25]

Monica also experiences a "conversion," from worldly ambitions to joyfully following God's plans for her and her son.

---

[24]Ibid., 296: "At no point in his account about Monnica's life does Augustine's mother look so unendearing ... The description of the separation also bears all the marks of Monnica's handiwork. However one looks at it, Augustine points the finger of blame at Monnica first, and at himself second." Cf, Kate Cooper, *Queens of a Fallen World: The Lost Women of Augustine's Confessions* (London: Basic Books, 2023), 48: "This makes Monnica's firm hand in dismissing her [Augustine's concubine] seem more understandable, though no less brutal."

[25]*Conf.* 8.12.30. Cf. Asiedu, "Following the Example of a Woman," 277: "In the moment of resolution for her son, Monnica too undergoes a conversion: her mourning is turned into a joy that is purer and more chaste, a joy that is not tied to earthly cares and hopes."

A not inconsiderable payoff to this line of analysis is that it makes more and different sense of the contrast or opposition between Monica and the concubine. As noted, they and their interests are set in opposition in the scene in which Augustine (he claims under Monica's influence) dismisses the concubine. As above—if Monica (good) is usually presented by way of contrast with Augustine (bad), here the concubine (extra bad) stands in as the epitome or personification of Augustine's worst, most fleshly and sinful urges,[26] which Monica helps him reject.[27] But if the portrayal of Monica herself is ambiguous, and she shares the deepest, most sinful desires with her son (ambition), then the deliberate contrast between Monica and the concubine is not between good and bad but between two women driven by their love for Augustine—one to cater to and foster his (and her) ambition, the other to fulfill his (and her) needs for companionship and intimacy, on the other. And in that contrast, Monica (at that point still deeply desirous of the social climbing outlined above) comes off as the worst.[28]

More importantly than this interpretation of the dismissal scene, it would also make the climactic conversion scene mean something quite different, or it would help us make sense of a problem I have had every time I've taught it for thirty plus years: I think Augustine is suggestive, maybe even ultimately quite unambiguous, that ambition is a far worse sin than lust, more dehumanizing, more damaging to oneself and to one's relationships. Yet he seems to make his climactic rejection of sin, his "conversion," a scene in which he renounces sexuality. (The scene in which he quits his career [*Conf.* 9.2.2] is not nearly as dramatic or prominent in the narrative. If not quite an afterthought, no one would mistake it for the most important turning point, in comparison to the garden scene.) We are then left struggling to explain (usually rather unconvincingly) how those two quite different kinds of renunciation or rejection relate to each other (even if we accept

---

[26] Cf. Miles, "Not Nameless," 168: "Indeed, the text's author, Augustine of Hippo, as well as numerous commentators across the centuries, present her briefly – if at all – as materializing specifically for the purpose of serving *his* passion" (emphasis in original).
[27] Thus Felicia McDuffie, "Augustine's Rhetoric of the Feminine in the *Confessions*: Woman as Mother, Woman as Other," in *Feminist Interpretations of Augustine*, edited by Judith Chelius Stark (University Park: Pennsylvania State University Press, 2007), 97–118; see esp. 98: "I will use the passages above as reference points from which to explore Augustine's representations of woman and the feminine in the *Confessions*. This examination reveals that while the figure of woman as mother plays a significant and positive role in the work, the shadow figure of woman as 'other' plays an equally significant but more ambiguous part."
[28] Cf. Asiedu, "Following the Example of a Woman," 296: "On the scale of imperfection Monnica seems to be at the high end with Augustine somewhere in the middle."

the unexpectedly different prioritization of them). But in a really brilliant unpacking of the scene, it can be shown that lust is, as we suspected, the less bad sin, and the climactic change of will is Augustine's rejection of his ambitious, sinful goals for himself, and his sorrowful repentance at the pain he caused while pursuing such destructive, sinful, selfish ends:

> As he saw things in hindsight, the problem he had faced in the summer of 386 was not that sex and marriage were obstacles to communion with God. Rather, it was that his *way* of pursuing them had been immoral.
>
> On this reading, the received view is not wrong that Augustine was recoiling from sin when he decided not to marry. But the sin that repulsed him was not lust; it was greed. What shook him, finally, was his willingness to betray the woman who *ought* to have been his wife – the mother of his child – for a lucrative arranged marriage. The root of his problem was not sexual desire. It was ambition.[29]

The drama and pathos of the scene would be worthy of Augustine as a showman, a rhetorician, regardless—but now I think we have an interpretation that is worthy of him as a humane and moral thinker. The scene, then, is not just dramatic, it is logically consistent with his moral analysis as developed throughout *Confessions*.

Monica's joy in the aftermath of Augustine's conversion moves her depiction from contrast to comparison or equivalence: both she and Augustine have overcome their sinful urges, rejected sinful lives, and committed themselves to following God. And following God has the more specific implication of trusting themselves to God's care and guidance, relying on God and fulfilling his demands,[30] rather than following their own desires. This is the real, full resolution to the problem stated in the opening paragraph of *Confessions*—that no desire can fulfill humans or offer them rest, except to desire God and what He wills. Although much of *Confessions* works through contrast and conflict, it has always had unity and convergence as the goal of its characters, and Augustine's conversion brings such peace to both him and his mother.

---

[29]Cooper, *Queens of a Fallen World*, 182; emphases in original.
[30]Cf. Haste, "So Many Voices," 8: "Her legacy commends to future generations not a divine strength inherent to the office of motherhood, but rather the incredible way that God can use someone devoted to himself and his purposes."

The resolution with the concubine—though not as complete and satisfying as that between Augustine and Monica—is a similar movement from contrast with sinful Augustine to agreement with converted Augustine. When the concubine is dismissed, she vows sexual renunciation, while Augustine—already engaged but unable to wait until the marriage—immediately finds another sexual partner with whom to occupy himself. Augustine presents it as another vice and weakness of himself, in contrast to the "example" set by the concubine, that he is too weak to follow:

> Meanwhile my sins were multiplying, for the woman with whom I had been cohabiting was ripped from my side, being regarded as an obstacle to my marriage. So deeply was she ingrafted into my heart that it was left torn and wounded and trailing blood. She had returned to Africa, vowing to you that she would never give herself to another man, and the son I had fathered by her was left with me. But I was unhappy to follow a woman's example. I faced two years of waiting before I could marry the girl to whom I was betrothed, and I chafed at the delay, for I was no lover of marriage but the slave of lust. So I got myself another woman, in no sense a wife, that my soul's malady might be sustained in its pristine vigor or even aggravated, as it was conducted under the escort of inveterate custom into the realm of matrimony.
>
> The wound inflicted on me by the earlier separation did not heal either. After the fever and the immediate acute pain had dulled, it persisted, and the pain became a cold despair.[31]

And Augustine's conversion in Book 8 enables him then to follow her example and take upon himself the same denial and rigors that she had already embraced. (Though of course we are denied witnessing any rejoicing from her, if there was any, or if she even knew Augustine's subsequent life, so it is not exactly equivalent to Monica's resolution and conversion described in Book 8.) It is even possible—I might say rather tempting in its equivalence—that she joined a religious community before Augustine joined one, and thereby she further anticipated the more deliberate choices he would later make.[32]

---

[31]*Conf.* 6.15.25.
[32]Cf. Miles, "Not Nameless," 183:

A further difference between Monica and the concubine is that Monica accompanied Augustine and his male friends to Cassiciacum (*Conf.* 9.4.7)[33] and is recorded as a participant in the dialogues Augustine wrote there, his earliest surviving writings. Besides their interest as witnessing an earlier stage in Augustine's thought, they also provide a salutary balance to the presentation in *Confessions*. Because of when he composed *Confessions*, and the kind of text it is (a prayer to God),[34] it often feels like Augustine is on a solitary, intellectual quest—alone with his thoughts, introspectively examining his feelings and actions, silently studying difficult texts—and after pages of detailed description of prayer and meditation, the reader is only afforded glimpses that remind her that Augustine lived most of his life, not alone in his study or under a pear or fig tree, but in lecture halls and dining rooms, conversing and interacting with others.[35] The dialogues give us an insight into this more social, communal activity that was, at the time, how his philosophical quest or his life as a philosopher was really lived.[36] One learns best through dialectic, through the give and take of dialogue,

---

We do not know whether she returned to North Africa to live in a religious community as Augustine did somewhat later. Let us conjecture that she did, for that is the only option offered by her society that would have permitted her to concentrate on the very aspect of her life that is most conspicuously missing in Augustine's *Confessions*, namely, her subjectivity.

She is followed somewhat more emphatically by Bouwman, 54: "She returned to North Africa and became 'voluntary widow' in the service of the local Catholic community ... She was an example for Augustine, because he had not yet made a choice for Christian Faith."

[33]Though Cooper, *Queens of a Fallen World*, 194, notes that, given the invisibility but sometimes ubiquity of female characters in Augustine's text, there may have been other women at the retreat: "Other women are not mentioned, but this does not guarantee that they were not present."

[34]Cf. Djuth, "Augustine, Monica, and the Love of Wisdom," 227: "Because the emphasis in the *Confessions* is on recollection more so than on dialectical reasoning into the truth, Augustine's perception of Monica reflects to a great extent how her character appeared to him prior to his conversion."

[35]Cf. Djuth, "Augustine, Monica, and the Love of Wisdom," 221: "It is against the background of these experiences that Augustine composes the Cassiciacum dialogues shortly after his conversion. Like Cicero and Socrates before him, in these dialogues he intends to pursue the philosophical life, but now as a Christian in the company of friends and relatives, among whom he includes his mother Monica."

[36]Cf. Douglas Finn, "The Holy Spirit and the Church in the Earliest Augustine: An Analysis of the Character of Monnica in the Cassiciacum Dialogues," *Papers Presented at the Seventeenth International Conference on Patristic Studies* 24 (2017): 141–65, esp. 164: "In all of this Augustine will come to emphasize, to one degree or another, that ascent to a vision of the Triune God is not a purely rational, inward, and individual affair, but an outwardly oriented and communal process of spiritual reformation that is never complete in this life."

and in humble inquiry with others, how to live and follow a life that values spiritual and not just earthly, physical realities.[37]

This would impress on students of Augustine, how important it is to have his philosophy in dialogue form, and not just as finished, settled conclusions he contemplated years later in *Confessions*, as he prayed to God. But that Monica would play as central a role in the dialogues as she does is a further insight. She is not incidental or peripheral—though Augustine, the other dialogue participants, and Monica herself, all express surprise at a woman being so prominent in such a discussion.[38] At first, she seems to be a helper or spokesperson, there to set things up or facilitate moving the conversation along, so the master Augustine can give the authoritative answer to the point under discussion: "Monnica appears often in Augustine's early philosophical dialogues as an alter ego who sums up the substance of what the others are trying to say, occasionally catching his eye and asking a useful question that will help someone who is struggling to understand. At Cassiciacum, the complicity between the two is evident but understated."[39] But as the conversation progresses, Augustine has to acknowledge Monica plays a greater role in the inquiry: something in her responses is as necessary (if not more so) to the success of their mutual philosophical endeavor, as his knowledge and study of philosophy, which she of course lacks. What comes out of these dialogues seems to be that in order for one to learn or advance

---

[37] Ibid., 158: "The philosophy Augustine attributes to his mother is strongly marked by the practice of worldly renunciation ... Even so, there is ... resistance to any utter denigration of the world ... reminders of the institutional church and its authoritative teachings, even of the physical building for which Monnica and others risked their lives."

[38] Cf. Clarissa W. Atkinson, "'Your Servant, My Mother': The Figure of Saint Monica in the Ideology of Christian Motherhood," in *Immaculate & Powerful: The Female in Sacred Image and Social Reality*, edited by Clarissa W. Atkinson, Constance H. Buchanan, and Margaret R. Miles. The Harvard Women's Studies in Religion series (Boston: Beacon Press, 1985), 139-72, esp. 143:

> At Cassiciacum, where Augustine and some companions retired after his conversion to read and study and talk, she was not simply an honored guest (or a housekeeper) but a participant in the conversation of her son and his friends. Augustine said that Monica reached 'the very height of philosophy' during a discussion of the good life. The company, 'forgetful completely of her sex, believed some great man was seated with us'. In another dialogue, Monica herself commented that women were not usually included in philosophical discussions or mentioned in books of philosophy.

[39] Cooper, *Queens of a Fallen World*, 203. Cf. Djuth, "Augustine, Monica, and the Love of Wisdom," 222: "Augustine, therefore, seems to relegate Monica to the subordinate position of a student who is not well-versed in philosophical matters but who, like the other participants in the conversation, is willing to learn."

the conversation, a higher IQ and greater level of knowledge are not the only or most necessary requirements: one must want to learn and love the source of knowledge (God)—and that eager, humble, loving attitude is what Monica brings to the conversation, so much so that Augustine acknowledges her as a better philosopher than he himself.[40] This seems to settle the question with which *Confessions* began, as to whether knowing or praising God is the more necessary or fundamental step (*Conf.* 1.1.1): Monica's devotion to God makes her the student most capable to learn more about Him, while Augustine's greater level of knowledge only fills him with anxiety and doubt that for years frustrate his attempts to learn more about Him or praise Him.[41]

As surprising but fulfilling as the dialogues are to Augustine's philosophy, the climactic scene of Monica's accomplishments and potential as a lover of wisdom, a philosopher, a senior companion helping Augustine draw closer to God along with herself, is much more ecstatic and mysterious. This is the vision at Ostia, the most dramatic and pivotal scene in *Confessions*, other than the conversion scene in Book 8. Augustine describes that there, standing on a balcony, he and his mother discourse together. Their mutual discussion and exploration raise the awareness and understanding of them both ever higher—through created things, through their own minds, to the contemplation of Being itself:

> Our colloquy led us to the point where the pleasures of the body's senses, however intense and in however brilliant a material light enjoyed, seemed unworthy not merely of comparison but even of remembrance beside the joy of that life, and we lifted ourselves in longing yet more ardent toward *That Which Is*, and step by step traversed all bodily creatures and heaven itself, whence sun and moon

---

[40]Cf. Djuth, "Augustine, Monica, and the Love of Wisdom," 222: "Yet, as the conversation proceeds, it is Monica, not Augustine, who intuitively resolves the dilemmas concerning the philosophical life and Augustine who must concede that she is indeed a true philosopher and a better one at that than he is."

[41]Cf. Djuth, "Augustine, Monica, and the Love of Wisdom," 232:

> Augustine portrays Monica in the way in which he does, then, because he recognizes that it is only by humble devotion to God that the return to God is possible. If Augustine emphasizes different aspects of Monica's character in the Cassiciacum dialogues and the *Confessions*, it is because he recognizes in these works that Monica's love of wisdom at Cassiciacum was far more mature than his was on account of his pride in learning, and that God had a way of making this evident to him through the aid he bestowed on Monica and the quickness with which she grasped the truth.

and stars shed their light upon the earth. Higher still we mounted by inward thought and wondering discourse on your works, and we arrived at the summit of our own minds, and this too we transcended, to touch that land of never-failing plenty where you pasture Israel for ever with the food of truth. Life there is the Wisdom through whom all things are made, and all others that have been or ever will be; but Wisdom herself is not made: she is as she always has been and will be for ever. Rather should we say that in her there is no "has been" or "will be," but only being , for she is eternal, but past and future do not belong to eternity. And as we talked and panted for it, we just touched the edge of it by the utmost leap of our hearts; then, sighing and unsatisfied, we left the first-fruits of our spirit captive there, and returned to the noise of articulate speech, where a word has beginning and end. How different from your Word, our Lord, who abides in himself, and grows not old, but renews all things.[42]

They are able to hold on to this vision briefly and with great enjoyment or ecstasy, before the exigencies of physical existence (sounds and sensations) draw them back to their ordinary existence, though Augustine recalls it years later, and memorializes it as the climactic ending of the autobiographical section of *Confessions*.

As in my description of the social aspect of the dialogues, the vision at Ostia is the ultimate validation and instantiation of how one shares the knowledge one can only attain by seeking together with others. The scene is an idealized, focused depiction of the action and relationships portrayed more sporadically in the dialogues, distilled into one very memorable vignette.[43] Augustine briefly could ascend to a vision of the divine in Book 7, but it was incomplete and frustrating, both because of the content but also because of the company, or lack thereof—Augustine was alone. The conversion in Book 8 is more of a breakthrough, because of the content, and because Augustine's will as well as his understanding turns and is converted—but it is still solitary and fleeting. The vision at Ostia is the final word, the real achievement of a blessed state, because it is achieved simultaneously by multiple visionaries in

---

[42] *Conf.* 9.10.24.
[43] Cf. Ragnar Holte, "Monica, 'the Philosopher,'" *Augustinus* 39 (1994): 293–316, esp. 297: "The *otium* at *Cassiciacum* represented a new attempt to realize a dream he had born for 13 years: the dream of a common life in constant search for wisdom, shared by several brethren of the same mind."

cooperation, working and seeking together:[44] "Monica's participation in the vision at Ostia along with Augustine manifests the ability of both to attain the most profound love of wisdom possible in this life. The emphasis on the social aspect of salvation that permeates Augustine's works finds its fruition in the shared vision at Ostia."[45] But to emphasize, as we here consider its implications for how women, specifically, are depicted in *Confessions*: all of this could have been done with a story of Augustine and one of his male fellow philosophers/believers engaging in such a discourse and attaining such a vision. So the fact that it is a woman, Monica, adds some further insight, or else Augustine would have written the scene differently, with different details and characters.

What it finally amounts to is that the climactic scene of *Confessions*—the climactic scene of rightly, fully seeking and praising God that fulfills the longing with which the book began—is only possible because of Monica and the kind of believer she is.[46] And this is despite Augustine sharing many of the assumptions of female inferiority that were prevalent (basically ubiquitous) in antiquity.[47] But Monica's story can transcend Augustine's limitations because throughout he focuses on her as mother, as having generated him: the climactic resolution of his story must include the one who generated him, his mother, as together they see their ultimate Source, God.[48]

To summarize: Augustine is rather famously limited by his historical context (as are we all). This would include in his attitudes toward women, whom he would have assumed to be intellectually inferior to men. But in the case of Monica, and maybe even based on his experience with the

---

[44]Though cf. J. Kevin Coyle, "In Praise of Monica: A Note on the Ostia Experience of *Confessions* IX," *Augustinian Studies* 13 (1982): 87–96, who argues the vision is Monica's, not Augustine's (or at least the emphasis or importance is on her, not him).

[45]Djuth, "Augustine, Monica, and the Love of Wisdom," 231.

[46]Cf. Atkinson, "Your Servant, My Mother," 143: "More was involved than inclusiveness, which did not much concern Augustine or his colleagues. They were concerned about faith, and in the *Dialogues* of Cassiciacum, Monica is not simply herself, but the representative of uneducated Christians whose faith might be more valuable than the learning of philosophers."

[47]Cf. Anne-Marie Bowery, "Monica: The Feminine Face of Christ," in *Feminist Interpretations of Augustine*, edited by Judith Chelius Stark (University Park: Pennsylvania State University Press, 2007), 69–95, esp. 76: "Although remarks about the inferiority of women pervade the Augustinian corpus, Augustine's treatment of Monica suggest that a woman can attain the same intellectual and spiritual insights about divinity as men."

[48]Cf. Virginia Burrus and Catherine Keller, "Confessing Monica," in *Feminist Interpretations of Augustine*, edited by Judith Chelius Stark (University Park: Pennsylvania State University Press, 2007), 119–45, esp. 120:

concubine as having birthed and nursed and helped raise their child,[49] he sees a receptivity to God, a humble acceptance of truth, that draws her closer to Him more quickly and easily than her intelligent but arrogant son can find a way.[50]

> But perhaps we make too much of his sheer originality, his autogenerativity? We forget – or fail to notice – that it is his mother who provides him the narrative material out of which to conceive time and space, to frame the very cosmos. Monica's life (centered on her death) gives him his opening, keeps his story of conversion open. Monica is Augustine's eternally unfinished business; she is present in all his beginnings.

[49]Suggested by Bouwman, "Spiritual Motherhood," 67:

> During the vision of Ostia, Monnica's mediation was transformed into a direct experience of God simultaneously with Augustine. This revelatory experience formed a literal inclusion. Augustine was introduced to revelatory experiences at the start of his life, in which Monnica was an instrument of divine consolations. Then towards the end of her life, they received the gift of grace together from the Divine Source. Augustine possibly reconstructed this connection with the help of his mistress' testimony, who nursed his son.

[50]Carnes, *Motherhood*, 20, also sees in the connection between mother and nursing child, not a vivid illustration of sin, as in *Conf.* 1, but an inkling of the longing to return to God: "Your desire for milk is excessive – and in that excessiveness, the desire points beyond itself. It suggests a desire that has not yet found its end."

CHAPTER 4
WOMEN IN *KING LEAR*

In reviewing the female characters in *King Lear*, I am again interested really in something quite narrow and purely literary: What do the dialogue and actions of the character, King Lear, reveal about his attitude toward women? This is as close as possible to the examination done in the previous chapter, given that in *Confessions* we had the somewhat more complicated situation of a character who is also the author. The same limitations or specifications should be repeated here, as in that chapter: I am not trying to come up with a general theory of Shakespeare's attitude toward women, nor a historical reconstruction of the real lives of women in Elizabethan England, though both of those larger projects may touch peripherally on my more modest endeavor.

To start: the character's attitude toward women is so extremely negative that most of our examination can be narrowed to considering specifically "misogyny" in *King Lear*, rather than the broader and more neutral "attitude towards women."[1] The character's speeches about women are so violently hostile and at times even obscene, expressing not just dislike or disapproval but physical revulsion, that it has led to the speculation that Shakespeare himself must have had some horrible, negative experience with women at the time he was writing the play—specifically, that he had contracted syphilis.[2] In a way, this combines both of the kinds of analysis I'm trying to avoid into one single speculation: a general theory about Shakespeare and a reconstruction of the historical situation. So I am not endorsing this interpretation, nor basing mine on it, but noting it at the beginning of

---

[1] Though cf. Philippa Kelly, "See What Breeds about Her Heart: *King Lear*, Feminism, and Performance," *Renaissance Drama* 33 (2004): 137–57, esp. p. 138, for the caution "that misogyny in *King Lear* is less the property of the play than that of gender-inflected ideas and terminologies imposed by critics." She goes on to examine many recent performances of *King Lear*, highlighting where "feminist perspectives are mindful of, and interested in, differences – in representation, in interpretation – involving women" (p. 139).

[2] See David Sanderson, "Why Shakespeare Had Woman Trouble," *The Times*, October 10, 2018, p. 23. https://www.thetimes.com/article/shakespeare-s-misogyny-may-be-explained-by-his-syphilis-7xsh8mc0j (accessed May 19, 2025).

my examination, since it is based almost entirely on the text of *King Lear*, with some confirmation from Shakespeare's biography (i.e., that he was at court less than other actors during the time in question), and references in the sonnets to mercury baths (a supposed treatment for syphilis at the time). Since Shakespeare's plays include many other depictions that could be considered misogynistic (e.g., a character named as a "shrew" in need of "taming"), it is worth noting that the misogyny of *King Lear* stands out as so unrestrained and excessive, that it is this play that makes people suspect its author's brain was being eaten up with syphilis. And it is the play, not just the character, which is influenced by misogyny, because Goneril and Regan themselves are creations of Shakespeare, and are modeled as horrific, exaggerated fantasies of how Elizabethan men imagined evil women.[3] All of this forms another point on which comparison with Donald Trump has been too tempting for many to resist—or really, equating Trump with Lear has been reinforced by speculating both Trump and Lear's creator, Shakespeare, were syphilitic.[4] Productions of *King Lear* during the first Trump presidency (2016–2020) often alluded to Trump by shaping their depiction of Lear to remind theater goers of the then (and now future) President;[5] now that we are going to be ruled by Trump again, we will have to see if that again shapes interpretation of the play.[6]

In considering Lear's attitude toward women, it is also worth noting that we have a very different situation than what we had when considering

---

[3] Cf. Novy, *Love's Argument*, 153: "Goneril and Regan are much less pyschologically complex than most Shakespearean characters of comparable importance. Few of their lines carry hints of motivations other than cruelty, lust, or ambition, characteristics of the archetypal fantasy of the woman as enemy."

[4] The similarity to Lear was suggested during Trump's presidency—for example, Anna North, "President Trump's King Lear Moment," *New York Times*, May 17, 2017 (online at https://www.nytimes.com/2017/05/17/opinion/president-trumps-king-lear-moment.html) and repeated since. The rumors of syphilis were recently revived: see Tom Norton, "Donald Trump Syphilis Rumors: Doctors Weigh In," *Newsweek*, January 19, 2024 (online at https://www.newsweek.com/donald-trump-syphilis-rumors-doctors-weigh-1861983).

[5] For example, in the 2019 Broadway production, starring Glenda Jackson as Lear, noted in the *Guardian* review: Alexis Soloski, "King Lear Review – Glenda Jackson Dominates Flawed Broadway Show," *The Guardian*, April 4, 2019, https://www.theguardian.com/stage/2019/apr/04/king-lear-shakespeare-glenda-jackson-broadway. I saw the resemblance there and in an amateur production in Rhinebeck, NY, in 2018.

[6] Though writing now in the immediate aftermath of the 2024 election, it would seem like my more progressive friends anticipate more dire repercussions for life in general. This could include the play, which was banned during the last ten year of the reign of George III: see Liz Armstrong, "*King Lear* Banned in England?" online at https://www.bard.org/news/king-lear-banned-in-england/.

Augustine's depiction of women in *Confessions*. With Augustine, we considered his mother and his romantic partner—two very specific kinds of relationships, and quite different from each other. And neither of those are available for us to consider with Lear, but only his attitude toward his grown daughters; he is not shown interacting with any other female characters. There is no relationship between characters that is the same between the two texts, on the issue of gender: Lear has no partner nor mother described in the text of the play, and Augustine has no daughter. The relative ages and the familial relationship are also completely different than in our previous chapter, and we must be careful that Lear's relating to other characters (however it is depicted) is affected by these factors other than gender.[7]

Further, and now that I begin unpacking the passages, I see this as the biggest hurdle to interpretation: it is possible for a character to say something hostile and derogatory to a female character without it being a symptom of general hostility toward women (misogyny). If a female character stabs another who shouts, "Stop, you fiend!"—that exclamation seems both provoked and commensurate, and the name used is gender neutral ("fiend"). It seems just an empty exclamation under duress. But it takes very little imagination to see how quickly that can become complicated, in scenarios where the provocation is less extreme than stabbing (e.g., asking someone with their hundred friends to make less noise, or be less demanding), and the insult hurled back may be gender specific or ambiguous. So each case would have to be individually analyzed and evaluated. And as I consider Lear's speeches to Goneril and Regan, I realize my sympathy is such for him, and my distaste for them is so extreme, that I could potentially excuse all his outbursts as justifiable or reasonable.[8] He's not a misogynist—as he says, he's a weak old man who's being disrespected and abused, and defending himself verbally, as his only remaining defense. Of course, as sympathetic as I am, I should also remind myself that he's been a tyrannical, narcissistic bully, as well as vengeful and petty, so if he blurts out hateful, sexist things afterward,

---

[7] Age is especially important: see Eonjoo Park, "Sympathy for Old Age in *King Lear*," *ANQ: A Quarterly Journal of Short Articles, Notes and Reviews* 34.3 (2021): 193–8. Cf. the similar analysis earlier by Wasserman, "And Every One Have Need of Other," 15–20.

[8] Cf. Novy, *Love's Argument*, 153: "Indeed, even if we follow Peter Brook's lead and imagine a Lear who knocks over tables, whose men really are a 'disordered rabble', their [Goneril and Regan's] cruelty to Lear and, even more, to Gloucester exceeds all provocation." Or cf. Bloom, *Invention of the Human*, 491: "The only woman in the play who is not a fiend is Cordelia."

they're not just meaningless syllables, but they may be expressions of a habitually hate-filled mind that is being exposed. So I could see that on the one hand, nothing may be misogynistic, if uttered by a sympathetic, abused, old man; but on the other hand, most everything may be misogynistic, if said by someone who's just been acting very badly.[9]

To go back to the observations that began this discussion (the speculations above on Shakespeare himself having syphilis): there is something subjective in this analysis. But not, I think, arbitrary. To say a passage is shocking or disturbing is not based on a mathematical calculation. But we have all felt it at certain passages—and even more so when seeing them enacted on stage. It is a feeling of, "I can't believe he went there." Or even, "I wish he hadn't said that." Maybe that captures our feelings best: we want to sympathize with Lear, but at several points, he goes too far in his hurt and rage, and we think, "Okay, I get that Goneril is a monster, but she didn't deserve *that*." And again—I know I've felt that when seeing it on stage, when the actor playing Goneril or Regan cowers or even sobs at the retaliatory abuse she has elicited from her father. As the kids say, "That was so cringe."

There are, I think, three such "cringe" passages—scenes where Lear reveals something ugly and monstrous about himself that is specific to how he relates to women (to give a fuller explanation now of misogyny): Act 1, scene 4 (with Goneril); Act 2, scene 4 (with both Goneril and Regan); and Act 4, scene 6 (in his final paroxysm of madness, to Gloucester). We will examine these closely, to try to get at what is distinctive or uniquely toxic about Lear's misogyny; we will also be sensitive to where and how it changes between these speeches.

To begin with the exchange from Act 1, scene 4:

LEAR	Degenerate bastard, I'll not trouble thee.
	Yet have I left a daughter.
GONERIL	You strike my people, and your disordered rabble
	Make servants of their betters.
Enter Albany.	
LEAR	Woe that too late repents!—⟨O, sir, are you come?⟩
	Is it your will? Speak, sir.—Prepare my horses.
	⌜ Some exit. ⌝

---

[9] And Novy, *Love's Argument*, 153, notes that Goneril herself genders her attacks on her own husband.

Ingratitude, thou marble-hearted fiend,
More hideous when thou show'st thee in a child
Than the sea monster!
[ALBANY Pray, sir, be patient.]
LEAR, ⌈to Goneril⌉ Detested kite, thou liest.
My train are men of choice and rarest parts,
That all particulars of duty know
And in the most exact regard support
The worships of their name. O most small fault,
How ugly didst thou in Cordelia show,
Which, like an engine, wrenched my frame of nature
From the fixed place, drew from my heart all love
And added to the gall! O Lear, Lear, Lear!
⌈He strikes his head.⌉
Beat at this gate that let thy folly in
And thy dear judgment out. Go, go, my people.
⌈Some exit.⌉

ALBANY
My lord, I am guiltless as I am ignorant
[Of what hath moved you.]

LEAR   It may be so, my lord.—
Hear, Nature, hear, dear goddess, hear!
Suspend thy purpose if thou didst intend
To make this creature fruitful.
Into her womb convey sterility.
Dry up in her the organs of increase,
And from her derogate body never spring
A babe to honor her. If she must teem,
Create her child of spleen, that it may live
And be a thwart disnatured torment to her.
Let it stamp wrinkles in her brow of youth,
With cadent tears fret channels in her cheeks,
Turn all her mother's pains and benefits
To laughter and contempt, that she may feel
How sharper than a serpent's tooth it is
To have a thankless child.—Away, away!

King Lear 1.4.263–303

The exchange begins with an invocation of illegitimacy, "bastard," with an added specification of "degenerate." And that follows up on the Fool's having raised that issue just a few lines earlier:

> FOOL   For you know, nuncle,
> The hedge-sparrow fed the cuckoo so long,
> That it's had it head bit off by it young.
> *King Lear* 1.4.220-2

"Cuckoo" being one of the animal images to invoke illegitimacy, and with implications much worse and less humorous than horns (the other, more frequent animal imagery of cuckoldry): the cuckoo lays its eggs in other birds' nests, where the intruder fledgling grows much faster than the other baby birds, until it murders and devours them, and then it devours its adopted parent.[10] Of course, that fits Lear's present situation of Goneril growing stronger than he is and able, physically, to overpower and subdue him. More importantly, however, it fits his imagination of what is happening: his daughters are not his—maybe not literally not his, but they are acting monstrous, inhuman (according to him). He cannot defend himself from Goneril's abuse, but he can disavow or disown her, as though she is of another species and not human. Most crucially, in his conception and how he describes it here, he thinks he bears no responsibility or connection to her behavior—it is all on her.

There follows a brief moment, when we think maybe Lear might admit his mistakes and take some responsibility: "Woe that too late repents." But that immediately goes back into blaming his daughters and not himself: "Ingratitude, thou marble-hearted fiend, More hideous when thou show'st thee in a child." And incidentally, since we are looking for misogyny—note how mollified Lear is in addressing Albany rather than Goneril throughout. Lear blames all his misfortunes on the women—not their husbands, nor himself—and even if he doesn't believe he's been cuckolded literally, to think of his daughters as metaphorically illegitimate is comforting to him and helps him avoid responsibility.

There follow some miscellaneous insults—"fiend," "sea monster," and "kite"—all inhuman and predatory creatures. And then a defense of the

---

[10] See Francisco Vaz Da Silva, "Sexual Horns: The Anatomy and Metaphysics of Cuckoldry in European Folklore," *Comparative Studies in Society and History* 48.2 (April 2006): 396–418.

proximate cause for this altercation (the behavior of Lear's entourage). Then, Lear gives one of the most absurd abdications of responsibility, by shifting all blame on to Cordelia: "O most small fault, How ugly didst thou in Cordelia show, Which, like an engine, wrenched my frame of nature From the fixed place, drew from my heart all love And added to the gall!" By this point in the play, the dishonesty and untrustworthiness of Goneril at least should be obvious, so to blame Cordelia for Lear now finding himself under Goneril's control seems absurd, and willfully overlooking the obvious.[11] It is an increasingly futile effort to insist, against mounting evidence, that Lear's outburst—and even the love test he began with—could have been a wise decision and course of action, if not for the variously ungrateful women. (And Lear himself will give his first indication that he realizes this, just a few lines later: "I did her wrong" [*King Lear* 1.5.21].) In particular, to say that it is Cordelia's "fault" that Lear, against his "nature," stopped loving her, sounds a lot like an abuser saying that the woman made him hit her (and I have seen at least one production in which Lear strikes Cordelia in the first scene, making such identification literal).

Lear now gives a particularly imprecatory "prayer." It is similar to how he will address the heavens in the storm scene but with a couple of important differences. Here, he addresses the higher power as "Nature, dear goddess," and he believes at this point she/it will do his bidding, obey his commands. He also maintains a certain balance in his conception of the universe, calling upon a female deity to aid him in his conflicts with a female (Goneril). He seeks to offset his misogyny not by aligning himself with a masculine force but by imagining a good (though vengeful) female deity on his side. And his commands are terrible curses upon Goneril, that she either be childless, or else suffer a child as ungrateful as she is (according to Lear). All of it is gendered, cursing her female body (e.g., "womb") and calling down punishments appropriate in Lear's mind as to what a female would suffer (e.g., tears) or find most painful (e.g., loss of youthful beauty).

---

[11] Cf. Elisa Oh, "Refusing to Speak: Silent, Chaste, and Disobedient Female Subjects in *King Lear* and The Tragedy of Mariam," *Explorations in Renaissance Culture* 34.2 (Winter 2008): 185–216, "The combination of silences and verbal competition to define them reproduces and reinterprets early modern discourses of femininity. By refusing to speak the politic words demanded by Lear's love test, Cordelia rejects the 'dishonesty' that is anathema to a good female political subject of patriarchy."

Given such an address, it seems appropriate to compare it to Edmund's soliloquy in Act 1, scene 2, as he also begins with "Thou, Nature, art my goddess" (*King Lear* 1.2.1), and though different in many specifics, the overall tone is similar. Lear and Edmund address a higher power as a "goddess," "Nature," to whom they complain bitterly of all the injustices done to them and seek redress through harming their family members, who they believe unfairly wield power over them and deny their rights. The two men are the most distant from each other in class and age and situation, but it seems strangely appropriate that both go to a "mother" figure to seek her protection,[12] though perhaps in oppositely equivalent situations. Lear is fantasizing a female deity or force of Nature to counteract the hostility heaped on him by females (his daughters), while Edmund fantasizes a kind and supportive female deity as a replacement for the neglectful and derisive male parent he has experienced in Gloucester.

Moving on to the next confrontation, which begins with Regan and moves to both sisters confronting their father:

> LEAR Regan, I think ⟨you⟩ are. I know what reason
> I have to think so: if thou shouldst not be glad,
> I would divorce me from thy ⟨mother's⟩ tomb,
> Sepulch'ring an adult'ress. ⌐ To Kent. ¬ O, are you free?
> Some other time for that.—Belovèd Regan,
> Thy sister's naught. O Regan, she hath tied
> Sharp-toothed unkindness, like a vulture, here.
> I can scarce speak to thee. Thou 'lt not believe
> With how depraved a quality—O Regan!
> REGAN I pray you, sir, take patience. I have hope
> You less know how to value her desert
> Than she to scant her duty.
> [LEAR Say? How is that?
> REGAN I cannot think my sister in the least
> Would fail her obligation. If, sir, perchance

---

[12] Cf. Sean K. Lawrence, "'Gods That We Adore': The Divine in *King Lear*," *Renascence* 56.3 (2004): 143–59, esp. 154: "... it is also symptomatic of Lear's – indeed of all the characters' – use of Nature as a transcendent sanction for their own positions. In this sense, Lear's Nature is not as different from Edmund's as is often assumed. Both characters invoke Nature to sanction their own selfhoods." But cf. Bloom, *Invention of the Human*, 483, who contrasts the two: "Neither of the drama's two antithetical senses of nature, Lear's or Edmund's, is sustained by a close scrutiny of the changes the protagonists undergo in Acts IV and V."

Women in *King Lear*

	She have restrained the riots of your followers,
	'Tis on such ground and to such wholesome end
	As clears her from all blame.]
LEAR	My curses on her.
REGAN	O sir, you are old.
	Nature in you stands on the very verge
	Of his confine. You should be ruled and led
	By some discretion that discerns your state
	Better than you yourself. Therefore, I pray you
	That to our sister you do make return.
	Say you have wronged her.
LEAR	Ask her forgiveness?
	Do you but mark how this becomes the house:
	⌜ He kneels. ⌝
	"Dear daughter, I confess that I am old.
	Age is unnecessary. On my knees I beg
	That you'll vouchsafe me raiment, bed, and food."
REGAN	Good sir, no more. These are unsightly tricks.
	Return you to my sister.
LEAR	⌜ rising ⌝ Never, Regan.
	She hath abated me of half my train,
	Looked black upon me, struck me with her tongue
	Most serpentlike upon the very heart.
	All the stored vengeances of heaven fall
	On her ingrateful top! Strike her young bones,
	You taking airs, with lameness!
CORNWALL	Fie, sir, fie!
LEAR	You nimble lightnings, dart your blinding flames
	Into her scornful eyes! Infect her beauty,
	You fen-sucked fogs drawn by the powerful sun
	To fall and blister!
REGAN	O, the blest gods! So will you wish on me
	When the rash mood is on.

King Lear 2.4.144–91

In this first section of the scene, we have some of the same elements as in the previous "cringe" scene above. It begins with Lear entertaining the possibility of illegitimacy and his wife's infidelity ("Sepulch'ring an adult'ress"). Lear calls down curses from heaven on Goneril, again specifying they attack her youth ("Strike her young bones"), and beauty ("Infect her beauty"). But as the daughters' sense of their own power increases, as well as their willingness to use it, Regan makes explicit what they are demanding: the daughters should be in charge, and Lear should accept this situation as just and reasonable ("You should be ruled and led By some discretion that discerns your state Better than you yourself"). The more he curses them, the more it shows how incompetent (even dangerous) and unable to control himself he is, and thereby justifies the daughters taking away their father's power, possessions, and freedom. And this of course increases and intensifies his curses, which further justifies their treatment of him, etc.

The form of Lear's curses changes, however, in his next longer speech:

LEAR   I prithee, daughter, do not make me mad.
       I will not trouble thee, my child. Farewell.
       We'll no more meet, no more see one another.
       But yet thou art my flesh, my blood, my daughter,
       Or, rather, a disease that's in my flesh,
       Which I must needs call mine. Thou art a boil,
       A plague-sore or embossèd carbuncle
       In my corrupted blood. But I'll not chide thee.
       Let shame come when it will; I do not call it.
       I do not bid the thunder-bearer shoot,
       Nor tell tales of thee to high-judging Jove.
       Mend when thou canst. Be better at thy leisure.
       I can be patient. I can stay with Regan,
       I and my hundred knights.
                                          King Lear 2.4.251–64

No longer is he calling down heavenly judgment or vindication ("I do not bid the thunder-bearer shoot"); he also seems to be reversing his earlier idea that Goneril is not his, but some alien creature (like the cuckoo). However, he is still not accepting responsibility but has come up with a more grotesque description that Goneril is a disease he must patiently suffer ("Thou art a boil, A plague-sore or embossèd carbuncle In my corrupted blood"), though he strangely raises the possibility of the relationship improving ("Mend when thou canst. Be better at thy leisure"). It is a peculiarly horrible, masculine version of how he relates to his progeny: rather than the maternal image of the child growing from her flesh, emanating from and extending herself, until it is viable and separate,[13] Lear instead conceives of Goneril like a tumor—or as above, like a lesion resulting from a venereal disease—growing inside him, eating away at him while erupting forth from his body, causing only pain and humiliation.[14] As the daughters seek to assert their power, they want their father to acknowledge the rightness of their claims, but this only intensifies the degree to which he feels victimized or persecuted by them.[15] As much as they are at odds, Lear and his daughters agree in thinking in very individualistic terms, that either Lear should be allowed to take care of himself, or the daughters should have total control over him: both are thinking in terms of power as binary and exclusive—either complete control or total submission. Unfortunately, neither is thinking of cooperation or community of shared or reciprocal responsibilities and burdens.[16]

---

[13] Cf. Carnes, *Motherhood*, 12: "I thought as a parent I would feel your infant presence as an extension of my own and that I would relate to you as my own body – or at least as flesh and blood I myself had produced, shaped, and molded."

[14] It is a fear and ambivalence of parents towards children: see Elizabeth Harper, "'A Disease That's In My Flesh Which I Must Needs Call Mine': Lear, Macbeth and the Fear of Futurity," *English Studies* 100.6 (2019): 604-26, esp. 605:

> In the tormented father (or would-be father) kings of King Lear and Macbeth, Shakespeare explores the violence and desolation that ensues when desire for self-sufficiency and oneness is forced to face the alterity of the child and the temporality it enshrines. Children represent the horizon of possibility and the motivating end of human endeavour, but their existence is also a reminder of the impossibility of totality. We are never truly masters of ourselves and can never truly be known to ourselves or to the Other.

Cf. Bidgoli, "Ethics, Subjectivity," 408, who notes "the inherently enigmatic and equivocal relationship between parents and children."

[15] As unnatural or monstrous as Goneril and Regan are, I don't think it follows that all modern attempts to overturn hierarchies are similarly unhealthy or misguided, or conversely, that any hierarchy is by definition good and just: cf. Mitchell Kalpakgian, "*King Lear*: The Attack on Fatherhood and the Destruction of Hierarchy," *Catholic Social Science Review* 3 (1998): 163-72., who connects the evil in *King Lear* with the "homosexual agenda" (p. 170) and "radical feminists" (p. 171), and concludes with the sweeping assertion that "If hierarchy is preserved, justice reigns" (p. 172).

[16] Cf. Harper, "A Disease That's in My Flesh," 605: "Lear and Macbeth cannot accept an existence that is shared by and dependent upon others who will go on in time beyond them; an existence that is predicated upon the unknowability of the future and upon acknowledging the need for human bonds to mitigate both the contingency of a hostile world and the condition of mortal embodiment." Also cf. Eonjoo Park, "Sympathy for Old Age in *King Lear*," *ANQ: A Quarterly Journal of Short Articles, Notes and Reviews* 34.3 (2021): 193-8, esp. 193: "Lear and his daughters seem to draw their attitudes toward old age from the commonplace views of the early modern era. Their reliance on these prevalent social notions ends up stressing individual responsibility at the expense of communal support and engagement."

But as much as Lear defaults to loudly proclaiming victimhood and a loss of power throughout the play, if he frames it as emasculation, as in his final speech before fleeing out into the storm, then it enrages him further, fuels his hatred of Goneril and Regan, and prompts statements of revenge or fantasies of a return to power:

> LEAR O, reason not the need! Our basest beggars
> Are in the poorest thing superfluous.
> Allow not nature more than nature needs,
> Man's life is cheap as beast's. Thou art a lady;
> If only to go warm were gorgeous,
> Why, nature needs not what thou gorgeous wear'st,
> Which scarcely keeps thee warm. But, for true need—
> You heavens, give me that patience, patience I need!
> You see me here, you gods, a poor old man
> As full of grief as age, wretched in both.
> If it be you that stirs these daughters' hearts
> Against their father, fool me not so much
> To bear it tamely. Touch me with noble anger,
> And let not women's weapons, water drops,
> Stain my man's cheeks.—No, you unnatural hags,
> I will have such revenges on you both
> That all the world shall—I will do such things—
> What they are yet I know not, but they shall be
> The terrors of the Earth! You think I'll weep.
> No, I'll not weep.
> I have full cause of weeping, but this heart
>   *Storm and tempest.*
> Shall break into a hundred thousand flaws
> Or ere I'll weep.—O Fool, I shall go mad!
>   *King Lear* 2.4.304–27

The scene is a crescendo of Lear's impotent rage or his enraged impotence. He returns to calling on the heavens ("You see me here, you gods"), but only to ask for the strength to keep himself from weeping, which he deems effeminate ("women's weapons," and which ironically, he just wished on Goneril). Better and more manly, in Lear's diseased (and at this point, definitely toxically masculine) mind, to fantasize an explosion of violence of which he is now completely incapable, against these "unnatural hags," than to weep for what is being done to him and for what he did to bring it about.

This inhumane refusal to weep, to hold on to a sanity based on falsity and denial, a perspective that falsifies what one sees and values things completely incorrectly—all this is what in the final "cringe" scene has driven Lear mad by its disconnect from the reality he now witnesses:

> LEAR Ay, every inch a king.
> When I do stare, see how the subject quakes.
> I pardon that man's life. What was thy cause?
> Adultery? Thou shalt not die. Die for adultery? No.
> The wren goes to 't, and the small gilded fly does
> lecher in my sight. Let copulation thrive, for
> Gloucester's bastard son was kinder to his father
> than my daughters got 'tween the lawful sheets. To
> 't, luxury, pell-mell, for I lack soldiers. Behold yond
> simp'ring dame, whose face between her forks
> presages snow, that minces virtue and does shake
> the head to hear of pleasure's name. The fitchew
> nor the soiled horse goes to 't with a more riotous
> appetite. Down from the waist they are centaurs,
> though women all above. But to the girdle do the
> gods inherit; beneath is all the fiend's. There's hell,
> there's darkness, there is the sulphurous pit; burning,
> scalding, stench, consumption! Fie, fie, fie, pah,
> pah! Give me an ounce of civet, good apothecary;
> sweeten my imagination. There's money for thee.
>
> *King Lear* 4.6.127–46

Throughout this scene, speaking to the blinded Gloucester, Lear spells out all the ways both men and women are loathsome, guilty, and hypocritical.[17]

---

[17] I had struggled to give a consistent interpretation to this scene, but was greatly aided by the analysis of Novy, *Love's Argument*, 155–256: "His words are anti-feminist commonplaces of Elizabethan England, but the context suggests a basis in revulsion against pretense and sexuality in general more than against women." Also cf. Bloom, *Invention of the Human*, 514: "Shakespeare, hardly a hater of women, risks this extremity precisely because Lear's troubled authority has foundered where he thought it most absolute: in the relationship with his own daughters ... so the mad king's revulsion is from nature itself, not an idea but the fundamental fact of sexual difference."

And right after this flurry of accusations that crescendoes to Lear retching at a woman's stench, he acknowledges that he himself reeks of mortality (*King Lear* 4.6.147)—an admission simultaneously of weakness, limitation, mortality, and femininity.[18] Rather than railing against human evil, or impotently decrying it, or playing the innocent victim of it, Lear finally acknowledges his place and role in the lineage of evil.[19] Though he had earlier entertained the misogynistic, self-pitying fantasy that like the cuckoo, Goneril and Regan are not his progeny, but rather murderous aliens; such a self-serving fantasy of victimhood now is specifically denied by facing reality ("got 'tween the lawful sheets"). But their cruelty and selfishness are generalized to all women as predatory and lustful as the mythological, part human and part animal "centaurs." Lear's misogyny that began as very specific accusations against his daughters—accusations that left him as unindicted, or indeed, innocent—is now universalized in his madness to describe the whole human race, but without the anger, revenge, or self-pity that characterized his earlier speeches cursing Goneril and Regan. And that final point is all that gives this scene any hope—that abandoning his own self-pity and owning his own guilt is the biggest and most difficult step toward potential honesty and healing: "They told me I was everything. 'Tis a lie" (*King Lear* 4.6.123-4).

Besides this final outburst of madness, Lear's "regular" misogyny contains many of the elements typical of misogyny throughout history. It includes (or at least acknowledges the fearful possibility of) the male terror of being cuckolded and the possible illegitimacy of his children. This fear then metastasizes or expands to be general, human anxiety over losing one's potency (or even more broadly, one's agency and freedom).[20] Such anxiety at a hostile world can be focused and blamed on females as those supposedly robbing one of his power (with castration being the most violent and extreme version of such), as it is here with Goneril and Regan (and even at first on Cordelia, for disobeying and thereby undermining and diminishing

---

[18] Cf. Novy, *Love's Argument*, 157: "Just after Lear gags at imagining the stench beneath women's girdles, he acknowledges the smell of mortality on his own hand."
[19] Ibid.: "From this vision of universal guilt, Lear moves to a vision of universal suffering, the basis for a different kind of mutuality."
[20] The female villains are also shaped by this dynamic because Goneril and Regan seem motivated by a fear of losing power. See Novy, *Love's Argument*, 154: "Here the play suggests that weakness, or the fear of it, can be as corrupting an influence as power. The fear of weakness is, however, a standard enough trait in the psychology of violence that it does little to individualize them [Goneril and Regan]."

Lear's power). It can also expand to include any supposed weakness "forced" on males by females (e.g., weeping, or any emotional outburst), labeling it emasculation, no matter how much harm may be caused by restraining such expressions, or how much health and happiness may ultimately be gained by indulging in them. To guard against such loss of potency, the threatened male may call upon (or invent) a deity or natural force to protect his power and punish any females who threaten it, labeling them as unnatural or evil, unholy or monstrous.

To bring this back to where I began the analysis in this chapter: all of this happens as Goneril and Regan are—really, not in Lear's imagination—belittling him and increasingly taking away from him what little power he has left. So his misogyny is excessive and grotesque, but it is not gratuitous; until his final crescendo of madness (where it is also broadened to include men as well as women), it is not generalized to all women, either. All of this will help us understand his reaction to it and our evaluation of him.

It also helps us understand why the kind of blatant, over-the-top misogyny we have been examining is not in the very first scene. The horrible curses Lear pronounces on Cordelia in that scene are not gendered—he curses her as a supposedly ungrateful child, not as a woman. And he focuses entirely on his own feelings ("Here I disclaim all my paternal care," *King Lear* 1.1.125)—which is, in his mind, the right retaliation here: he offered her the best share of everything (land and power), and she spurned it (to his mind), so he withdraws the offer; she broke the bond of obedience, so he breaks the parental bond of "care." It is an assertion of power and ugly in his abuse of it. Likewise, in the first scene, Goneril and Regan appear to submit, so Lear rewards them, as they have (to his mind) appropriately affirmed his power. In the scenes we've examined above, Lear had given Goneril and Regan all the power, and it was they who broke all bonds with him: his misogynistic retaliation therefore is an expression of impotency and powerlessness.

The extent to which the contest with which Lear begins the play is itself based on misogynistic assumptions is harder to determine. I am trying to be as generous to him as possible, viewing the division of the kingdom as sincerely done with an eye toward peace and stability ("that future strife May be prevented now," *King Lear* 1.1.47–8), and given Goneril and Regan's subsequent behavior, this seems quite reasonable. To base such division on a public, verbal acclamation of deeply personal, private feelings, especially when Goneril and Regan also seem eminently capable of deceit and flattery (while Cordelia is utterly inept at such), seems much less shrewd, to say the least, but it need not be gender-based: sons as well as daughters could be asked to state their love and show their obedience;[21] even subjects and not just children could have such a demand put on them, with possibly similarly disastrous results. Further, if as described above, misogyny such as Lear expresses, comes from a male who is feeling (or fearing) a loss of power and blames it on women, then it would make sense that Lear's first outburst is not misogynistic, since at that point he still has power and is wielding it against all his progeny.

---

[21] One of the most famous and successful adaptations of *King Lear*, Akira Kurosawa's *Ran* (1985), has sons rather than daughters as the three children.

CHAPTER 5
CONCLUSION

Powerfully Present

I move in this concluding chapter to consider the outcome or resolution of what I have examined. Not the historical outcome of *Confessions* and Augustine's life (where he becomes the powerful and successful bishop of Hippo and dies many years after the events he narrates in *Confessions*); and not the narrated ending of *King Lear*—in which, like all Shakespearean tragedies, most everyone (good or bad or indifferent) dies and horribly. I'm thinking more of an outcome that would respond to and build on what we have uncovered in these pages about the protagonists' relationship to power and the ultimate power (if any), God; and their attitudes toward and relationships with women. Having spent so long with our heroes (let me call them that here at the end, rather than the more neutral and non-committal "protagonists") through their journeys or ordeals, and considered them in such detail, how do we think they would ideally, if circumstances allowed, relate to God and women. Again—set aside that Lear is dead, and Augustine, historically, has whatever relations with God and women are recounted in his later works: take these "facts" as given and accidental and therefore not as interesting as what we have uncovered, or which Augustine and Shakespeare left for us to excavate. And that the Tate version of *King Lear* existed and was even the only version enacted on stage for much of the play's history[1] shows us the ending we've been studying is accidental and not necessary or inevitable. And for Augustine, although his surviving works are truly enormous—or really *because* he has left us so much writing to use as data for reconstructing his thought—his attitude toward women and what he really believed about God, at various points in his subsequent life, are still the objects of debate and interpretation. So, in either case, to state what "really happened" is not really possible, and perhaps not even as interesting

---

[1] See Jeffrey Kahan, "Introduction," in *King Lear: New Critical Essays*, edited by Jeffrey Kahan. Shakespeare Criticism, vol. 33 (New York: Routledge, 2008), esp. 14–19.

as we might initially have thought. But to ask, with the kind of familiarity and sympathy we have gained for our heroes after studying them so closely for so long, "Is there a moment, like Goethe has Faust speculate on and long for,[2] which would be how they would want things to be, and to continue indefinitely, if they could have it so?"—that seems both an interesting and answerable question, and one to which I now turn.

With the question stated thus, I think a surprising similarity emerges for me. As different as their stories and characters are, there is a moment for each of them when they are at peace, when they are no longer striving for anything but are just existing or resting in the presence of what and whom they love. Both are doing so with the woman they have disrespected and hurt previously, but to whom in this climactic scene, they are reconciled—though in both cases, and despite the preference throughout western literature for privileging a heterosexual couple as the center around which everything else revolves, it is not a lover or romantic partner, but a female blood relative.[3] For Augustine, this is the vision at Ostia, examined in Chapter 3. For Lear, it is in a brief scene as he and Cordelia are led off to be imprisoned (and in her case, murdered by Edmund's henchmen):

> LEAR
> No, no, no, no. Come, let's away to prison.
> We two alone will sing like birds i' th' cage.
> When thou dost ask me blessing, I'll kneel down
> And ask of thee forgiveness. So we'll live,
> And pray, and sing, and tell old tales, and laugh
> At gilded butterflies, and hear poor rogues
> Talk of court news, and we'll talk with them too—
> Who loses and who wins; who's in, who's out—
> And take upon 's the mystery of things,
> As if we were God's spies. And we'll wear out,

---

[2] See Johann Wolfgang von Goethe, *Goethe's Faust*, trans. by Walter Kaufmann (New York: Anchor Books, 1962) Part 1, "Night."

[3] This takes us back to a very primal model, the Oedipus story, as noted in comparison to *King Lear* by Geoffrey Bush, *Shakespeare and the Natural Condition* (Cambridge, MA: Harvard University Press, 1956), 96: "There are similarities between the stories of Oedipus and Lear. They are two old and angry kings divided from their kingdoms; Creon and Edmund follow the law of *physis*; unnatural children quarrel for the throne; and two faithful daughters bring restoration. And there is a similarity in what Oedipus and Lear discover about themselves."

Conclusion

> In a walled prison, packs and sects of great ones
> That ebb and flow by th' moon ...
>
> Upon such sacrifices, my Cordelia,
> The gods themselves throw incense. Have I caught thee?
> He that parts us shall bring a brand from heaven
> And fire us hence like foxes. Wipe thine eyes.
> The good years shall devour them, flesh and fell,
> Ere they shall make us weep. We'll see 'em starved first.
> Come.
>
> King Lear 5.3.9-20, 22-30

The formalities of their reunion have been attended to in Act 4, scene 7, where the ministrations of the doctor and Kent were acknowledged. More importantly—in that earlier scene, Lear's guilt and contrition are vividly described: "I am bound Upon a wheel of fire, that mine own tears Do scald like molten lead" (*King Lear* 4.7.52-4). He can "move on," not in the sense of forgetting or overlooking what he did and what has happened, but having fully experienced intense remorse and expiated such painful guilt.

This frees Lear to envision a future life with Cordelia as his vision of uninterrupted bliss—and not the "kind nursery" he had imagined at the beginning of the play (*King Lear* 1.1.138), which maintains his power by casting him as a tyrannical toddler and her as a (good, indulgent) mother,[4] but in a reciprocal, mutual, adult relationship. He does not imagine it as free, however—they are still, even in his imagination, imprisoned. He accepts the physical limitations of their existence, though he also imagines them overcoming normal boundaries, transcending or ignoring the passage of time that will still limit and even destroy everyone else outside their prison. The forgiveness he had asked for, and the blessing she had requested in the earlier scene, he now imagines as being done in response to one another, and as continuing on with other pleasant communications ("pray ... sing ... tell old tales ... laugh"), none of which will include tears or sadness. Lear

---

[4]Though cf. Marianne Novy, *Love's Argument: Gender Relations in Shakespeare* (Chapel Hill: University of North Carolina Press, 1984), 152:

> Elizabeth Janeway has explained how traditional expectations of female behavior come from nostalgia for a mother's care in childhood. Lear, in wishing to 'unburdened crawl toward death', wants to become a child still omnipotent in his ability to control Cordelia's 'kind nursery'. The illusory omnipotence of the abdicating king can be compared to the illusory omnipotence of the head of the family within his household.

here hearkens back to the opening scene of the play,[5] where his demand for speech elicited a refusal from Cordelia, but going forward, only free and joyful words will spill out of them both spontaneously and endlessly. Significantly, Lear here makes the only mention of "God" in the play (ambiguously, since "God's" and "gods'" are indistinguishable when spoken aloud), as ultimately in charge of their actions, and the "gods" as showing their approval and sanctification for the imprisoned but beatified life Lear imagines he and Cordelia will live together.

As noted, the casts of the two scenes (if one allows for there being bystanders in the *King Lear* version)[6] are the same—the male hero and the woman he loves but has previously wronged. What they experience is also similar in its unearthly, dream-like setting, going beyond the limits of the senses in *Confessions*, or beyond the constraints of time in *King Lear*. For Augustine and Monica, this leads to their experiencing divine Wisdom itself; in Lear's imagination, it is he and Cordelia experiencing themselves as "God's spies" and being affirmed by "the gods" (throughout the rest of the play, utterly silent and unresponsive to everything that goes on), as they learn "the mystery of things." Though given how the play ends, one has to label this scene a "hope" or even delusion of Lear's, while Augustine's is more real, given how things turn out, and can therefore be called a "vision"—I think both fulfill the criteria described above, that this is the moment the hero longs for, that if it could be fulfilled (and it's not in *King Lear* and even in *Confessions*, is so only briefly before Monica dies), this is his fondest longing and desire, that reveals what he really wants, believes in, and values.

Similar, too, are the obstacles or barriers our two heroes overcame to get to this moment. Throughout *Confessions*, Augustine constantly reminds us of the frequency and efficacy of Monica's tears, whereas his own emotions often failed him or were misdirected, up until this point—weeping excessively for his dead friend, or for the false spectacles of the theater. Now they together experience joyful equanimity, an ecstatic (literally, beyond the senses) vision.

---

[5]Cf. Brian Sheerin, "Making Use of Nothing: The Sovereignties of *King Lear*," *Studies in Philology* 110.4 (2013): 789–811, esp. 801: "What is more, lavish giving is actively contributive to Lear's version of sovereignty, augmenting (if I may use a Derridean pun) his royal presence precisely at the expense of his presents, his material loss."

[6]Though the recent production of *King Lear* by Kenneth Branagh considerably and oddly expands the scope and background of the scene, having Lear and Cordelia speaking to each other from opposite sides of the stage, with the bodies of those fallen in battle between them; it is one of many points wherein the production's emotional effect doesn't hit the right mark.

Conclusion

Lear similarly spends the entire play up until this moment either indulging in the excesses of emotion, especially rage and self-pity, while trying to deny normal, healthy expressions of how hurt he is, with his stubborn insistence that he will not weep. Cordelia, at the opposite extreme and similarly to Monica, is described as shedding particularly efficacious tears throughout.[7] After the release of the storm scenes, and the mutuality of the reunion scene with Cordelia, he too can express and sustain normal, healthy emotions, as painful as they are—and these especially include gestures and vulnerabilities typically associated with women.[8] I might normally say he has become more humane, integrated, and holistic, but in the context of this study, with its focus on the male hero's interactions with women, I think it is all right to say Lear has gotten in touch with his feminine side (as costly as that education has been) and can express not just a non-toxic masculinity but a human soul that is more balanced and self-aware and accepting of both masculine and feminine elements.[9]

As noted above in our analysis, both heroes needed to overcome their tendency to be domineering or demanding and to make themselves more humble and more accepting of others exerting power over them. This would also include no longer relying on typically masculine ways of thinking and understanding. In the case of Augustine especially, this would involve less reliance on reason and mastery to achieve either his "conversion" or the shared vision that follows it, and more on cooperation, intuition, and surrender. Both Lear and Augustine needed to overcome the baseline of

---

[7] Cf. Novy, *Love's Argument*, 158: "Nevertheless, it is remarkable both how often Cordelia's tears are mentioned in *King Lear* and how the imagery strives to make them powerful rather than pathetic."

[8] Cf. Novy, *Love's Argument*, 162-263:

> But when Lear enters with Cordelia dead in his arms, the visual image in itself suggests a change in him. The allusion to the pietà that many critics have seen here includes the fact that Lear is at this point taking on a posture much more characteristic of women than of men in our society – holding a child, caring for the dead ... Though he still clings to some of his traditional images of male and female virtues, when he says, 'Her voice was ever soft, / Gentle and low' (5.3.273-4), it is his own gentleness we see.

[9] Again cf. Bloom, *Invention of the Human*, 491:

> Are Shakespeare's perspectives in *Lear* incurably male? The only woman in the play who is not a fiend is Cordelia, whom some recent feminist critics see as Lear's own victim, a child he seeks to enclose as much at the end as at the beginning. Such a view is certainly not Cordelia's perspective on her relationship with her father, and I am inclined to credit her rather than her critics.

sexism in their societies to let themselves be open to the participation of a woman as an equal partner. For Augustine, this would have been more about overcoming both the tendency to undervalue, overlook, and discredit the intellectual abilities of women like Monica, as well as his own personal arrogance at overestimating his own intellectual abilities; for Lear, this would have been more a matter of abandoning whatever he is still clinging to self-defensively of a misogynistic attitude that fears women exerting and abusing power over him.

The final vision in each—in *Confessions*, of God; in *King Lear*, of a timeless love superior and impervious to all the pain, violence, and ugliness around it, that even transcends the imperfections of those participating in it—is stunning, literally breathtaking. It is shared not just between the characters but also between them and the audience or readers.[10] To be frank, it is the "high" I look for in any experience of the play on stage or any rereading of the texts—and though not every performance or reading takes one as high as every other, none leaves one unaffected. Both *Confessions* and *King Lear* present us with a love that goes beyond the particulars of the hero and his beloved, beyond the limitations of their social, biological, and gender roles,[11] and draws us in to participate in, or at least contemplate,[12] what such transformative love would be.

---

[10] Some actors now accentuate such breaking of the "fourth wall." See Nancy Selleck, "Interpersonal Soliloquy: Self and Audience in Shakespeare and Augustine," *English Literary Renaissance* 51.1 (2021): 63–95, esp. 68: the "point here is that the action of a Shakespearean soliloquy is always *partly about* the audience, so that the character is not just talking to the audience but engaging with them dialogically" (emphasis original).

[11] Cf. Gil, *Shakespeare's Anti-Politics*, 122:

> By the end of the play, the force of Lear's displacement from his social identity as king and father, and the force of Cordelia's displacement, is so great that the bond joining them is not a 'natural' bond of familial love. Indeed, if this were nothing more than a father-daughter reunion, it would be deprived of the haunting theatrical force that it has. In the love that joins Lear who was once a father and Cordelia who was once a daughter, in the love born of a profound sense of separation from the competition and status hierarchies of the social world, Shakespeare gestures toward a kind of love founded on the recognition of that ambivalent, luminescent substrate of social identity that I term the life of the flesh.

Similarly cf. Novy, *Love's Argument*, 158: "With Cordelia's tears, as with other aspects of her characterization, Shakespeare is suggesting a kind of power different from the coercion dependent on political rank or violence; it is the power of nurturing, of sympathy, of human connection as an active force."

[12] Cf. Novy, *Love's Argument*, 161:

Conclusion

I have tried to be more precise in this volume in distinguishing between Augustine's relentlessly theocentric vision and the ambiguous, more purely anthropocentric vision of *King Lear*. This occupied my analysis, especially in Chapter 2, in considering how enormously different would be a humility based on belief in God and one that is not. Here at the conclusion, allow me to sketch some of the points where the world views may intersect, or at least resemble each other. The first is to observe their similar effects, as I have tried to describe in their vision of what the heroes long for: whether one sees God or "just" the human beloved, one does so by going beyond societal roles,[13] by loving and prioritizing loves not based on their typical acceptance or the approval of others or how they assign value to them, as well as completely overcoming all ego. Overcoming such false priorities or loves, shattering such idols, is what occupies Lear in the difficult and painful middle of the play,[14] and what Augustine more gradually and less painfully overcomes in *Confessions*; for both, it is what makes the vision and transcendence described above possible.

In either world—Lear's ancient Briton or Augustine's fourth-century North Africa—loving, even to the point of seeing God, does not confer happiness or physical well-being in the present life. Even the hope with which it fills one is not about changing what is happening now, but about altering one's attitude toward current (and perhaps inescapable) events, as

---

Stanley Cavell has proposed that in *Lear* the inevitable separation between actors and audience mirrors the ultimate isolation of the characters, and all of us, from each other: we cannot stop the characters from acting wrongly, from suffering pain, just as they cannot stop each other, just as we cannot stop those closest to us. Yet, although Lear cannot save Cordelia, nor she him, before this ultimate loss he does experience her acceptance. This acceptance includes tragic perception – it is combined with knowledge of his faults. It does not condescend, but it supports Lear in his own willingness to acknowledge his limitations.

[13]Cf. Wasserman, "And Every One Have Need of Other," 29–30: "Kindness must be its own reward; and it can be, because it epitomizes the mutual bonds between all men which make society viable and existence bearable ... 'The entire point' for Lear, Kent, and the others, is simply that men must love one another above and beyond the duties and obligations demanded of them in their societal roles."

[14]Cf. Sean K. Lawrence, "'Gods That We Adore': The Divine in *King Lear*," *Renascence* 56.3 (2004): 143–59, esp. 153, 154:

Specifically, the gods are, for both Gloucester and Lear, abstractions of the principle of patriarchy ... Edmund's religion, like Lear's, is fundamentally a justification of his own agency and power ... As we have seen, however, the order of the heavens was a man-made construct in the first place. Demolishing it opens the possibility of 'true transcendence', as Levinas would say, beyond the idols.

painful as they are, as in Monica's ceasing to care when she dies or where her body will be laid. And Augustine is quite aware that the world around him offers and causes deaths far worse than the peaceful one Monica does, in fact, enjoy:

> [Augustine's] insistence on hope does not diminish his sense of the insufficiency of the here and now, however; if anything, it throws it into sharper relief. Listing in vivid detail "the calamities of this life" at the end of *The City of God*, itself written in the wake of the fall of Rome, Augustine concludes that our "state of life" is "so miserable that it is like a hell on Earth." When history comes to an end, there will be answers, but in the meantime we cannot make sense of tragedy: "We do not know" why the world is apparently devoid of justice.[15]

Such a view of the world as currently and unrelentingly grim but hopeful only in a promised but as yet unrealized future is wholly compatible with tragedy in general and *King Lear* in particular.[16]

In this concluding chapter and throughout, I have had to base my argument on things being compatible or comparable to one another, and my reasoning or analysis being likely or supported by the texts—I hope in ways that were convincing and compelling. But I want to underline at the end, that these texts are not the kinds that give certainty (even if Augustine wants his to be, or even pretends that it is). They are not essays or propositions. They are stories—even if both are, to varying degrees and in different ways, based on events that took place in human history. And that is exactly what gives them their power—that they are suggestive, evocative. We know

---

[15] Naomi Baker, "'This Sad Time': The Augustinian Temporality of *King Lear*," *Modern Philology* 120.3 (2023): 335–55, quotation on p. 337.
[16] Cf. Baker, "This Sad Time," 340, 355:

> The fact that *King Lear* explores relentless suffering, presenting history as an apparently shapeless, meaningless series of tragic events, has caused many critics to insist it is a secular or atheistic play, fundamentally opposed to Christian perspectives. Such accounts of *King Lear* often assume that Christian frameworks are incommensurate with those of tragedy. As Rowan Williams warns, however, 'It is very far from established that Judeo-Christian representations and tragic imagination must be regarded as incompatible ... In setting the stage for a happy ending that it then withholds, *King Lear* does not give the lie to Christian theology but instead gives powerful expression to the tragic temporalities in relation to which Christianity was forged. *King Lear* therefore presents a tragic vision of living in the senescence of the world, a temporal position characterized by agonized incomprehension and hope deferred.

Conclusion

immediately that we must try to say what they mean, that they must mean something, even as we are always aware that our attempts at explanation are incomplete and fall short. I think it is self-evident that the two texts treated here are meaningful, but their meaning is not self-evident. They demand a response, what we call interpretation, but it doesn't take much experience to see that people respond very differently to them, or even the same person changes their response over time.

A classic, extended essay on Shakespeare, *Shakespeare and the Natural Condition*, by Geoffrey Bush, makes this point in several ways, to several different effects.[17] Indeed, the essay itself seems to illustrate the point it is trying to make about Shakespeare: to read any paragraph of the essay is to make one nod in assent at its clear argumentation, to let oneself be mesmerized by such lucid prose. But then one catches oneself and wonders, "But what does it mean? How does it connect to what I just read elsewhere in the book?" I could pick out almost any sentence in the essay, and it would sound true and convincing, but I have difficulty picking out one that says, clearly and concisely, what the book is about, so I will have to quote a larger chunk from the middle of the essay:

> But in *Hamlet* and *King Lear* we witness the encounter between character and both aspects of nature, things and the meaning of things, the province of Bacon's philosophy and Spenser's. There is no constriction of the imaginative atmosphere in *Hamlet* and *King Lear*; there is instead, in Sir Thomas Elyot's phrase, a universal dissolution, and a constant crossing of things with their meaning. The damned souls of *Hamlet* and *King Lear*, Claudius and Edmund and Goneril and Regan and Cornwall, are not the protagonists; and what happens at the end to Hamlet and Lear cannot be called defeat. There are too many other possibilities; further meanings crowd upon the events; there is a continuous consciousness both of persons and events in themselves and of what they signify, and it is this double awareness of change and of what is beyond change that suggests a comparison between Bacon's exploration of things in themselves, Spenser's vision of a religious continuance beyond things, and Shakespeare's endeavor of the imagination.[18]

---

[17] Geoffrey Bush, *Shakespeare and the Natural Condition* (Cambridge, MA: Harvard University Press, 1956).
[18] Bush, *Shakespeare and the Natural Condition*, 75.

There are things (on stage, or that we read about), and there are the meanings of things; the former is usually clear and unambiguous, the latter is anything but. But it is the latter that is the most interesting and crucial to us in our lives and in these texts. The author here gives two examples of a specific outcome of what this describes—the endings of the two plays he thinks most clearly illustrate this problem. As every callow youth has summarized every Shakespearean tragedy: "Spoiler alert: everyone dies."[19] And it is not just the ending, but every crucial point in a text may be open to interpretation and therefore ambiguous.[20] Everything that happens in a play or text is simply a given and won't change, no matter how many times we read it or see it enacted.[21] But how we react to it, the meaning we ascribe to that event, differs between people, and between times that individuals encounter these texts. And besides changing, it may just remain ambiguous or impossible to state—specifically, in the two cases of the endings of *Hamlet* and *King Lear*, how we can say such universal suffering and destruction is not defeat, even as we also admit that what we can call it is not quite clear, either.

This ambiguity and changeability are much more clearly illustrated in a play like *King Lear*, of which we watch repeated productions precisely to experience more and different (and maybe even, we hope, better) meanings of the text. But there are enough varying interpretations of *Confessions* to show us that both the texts we've examined demand interpretation even as they resist unambiguous certainty, so much so that we can say interpretation and ambiguity are essential to their existence, meaning, and importance. Further, we could note that even in comparison to other playwrights, Shakespeare's ambiguity of meaning is remarkable, especially in *King Lear*,[22]

---

[19]Though I confess I hadn't realized or had forgotten that this is one of the differences between Ancient Greek and Shakespearean tragedy. See Bush, *Shakespeare and the Natural Condition*, 99: "Greek tragedy does not conclude with death; Orestes does not die at the end of the *Oresteia*, or Oedipus at the end of *Oedipus the King*. It is the Elizabethan tragic world that comes to an end in death, the simplest and most fundamental fact of the Elizabethan tragic vision."

[20]For example, cf. Wasserman, "And Every One Have Need of Other," 29, is a perfect example, in that he takes a specific exegetical point (Albany tells Edmund they are not brothers), and unpacks broader conclusions, then has to note that in a broader view, the play is ambiguous on these conclusions: "He shows the kind of wisdom in discrimination which Kent had revealed earlier, and which now offers some hope for an orderly, just future in the kingdom. Nevertheless, the conclusion is tonally ambiguous."

[21]Though, as a primarily text-based fan and critic, I have to remind myself that stagings of a play may differ enough to fundamentally change the meaning and experience of the play.

[22]Cf. Bush, *Shakespeare and the Natural Condition*, 10:

Conclusion

though it also seems to be typical of the pivotal and tumultuous time in which he lived.[23]

I will consider further the effects of such ambiguity in the epilogue that follows but let me acknowledge the problems (as seen and theorized by Augustine) before I do so. As someone who excelled at and profited by making spectacles, Shakespeare (as far as I know) did not provide a critique of his craft. If it could have been explained to him (or indeed, as he probably already knew, experientially), the observations above that people keep coming back to see a play, even if they know the ending; that they excitedly discuss it with their friends and argue over what they saw, or discuss how a given performance compared to another—all that would have struck him as intuitively obvious, and greatly to be encouraged, just for practical reasons of ticket sales, and the resulting fame and profit. But to turn to our other text for a critique: Augustine in *Confessions* and elsewhere articulates a deep unease with and suspicion at the consumption of imaginative literature, especially drama. And the ambiguity I have cited as a powerful literary and interpretive strength, something to be appreciated and celebrated, he sees as a sinful, damnable flaw. (And I call it "sinful" because Augustine would, but his criticism of course is pre-Christian, from as far back as Plato, so it is not a specifically "Christian" or even religious polemic, as the label "sinful" might imply.) The one critic cited above notes the theater's "ambivalent" portrayal of events and rightly calls that "seductive."[24] Augustine would completely agree on the label but would note that as part of his criticism: with fiction,

---

Certainly at the end of *Hamlet* and *King Lear* there is a sense of comfort, and of knowledge; something of great importance has been discovered about natural life. But what has been concluded, and what agreement has been reached? Nothing is said in *Hamlet* and *King Lear* that has the certainty of the knowledge offered by Shakespeare's two most distinguished contemporaries in the theater.

[23]Cf. Mitchell Greenberg, "The Concept of 'Early Modern,'" *Journal for Early Modern Cultural Studies* 13.2 (Spring 2013): 75–9, esp. 77, 78:

Perhaps the only cultural production that enables us to identify a unifying element in the enormous heterogeneity of what we are calling 'early modernity' is the almost universal predominance of the theater, its unrivaled status as the most popular and dominant form of representation during the most important transitory moment (1550–1700) in European history ... Rather than a mere representation of contemporary reality, theater questions that reality. Thus, in a sense, we can say that the theater is, and this is probably its most seductive appeal, inherently ambivalent ... In this ambivalence the theater would at one and the same time reflect the ambient confusion, essay different models of subjectivity and uphold and yet question the imposition of a political system.

[24]Greenberg, "The Concept of 'Early Modern,'" 78, cited above.

we willingly, gleefully and eagerly even, let ourselves be seduced, lied to, and according to Augustine (and Plato, and others), it is harmful both as to the deception, the willing surrender to it, and the content of the lie which we accept.

Natalie Carnes, in meditating on *Confessions* in her book *Motherhood: A Confession*, follows Augustine's critique. In an imaginary conversation with her infant daughter, she spells out the problem and how careful she is to not lead her daughter to "false" beliefs:

> What would it mean to pray for Antigone or Cordelia Lear? You often want to pray for your beloved blanket "Blankie" these days. Part of you, though I don't think all of you, believes Blankie is alive because you love her so much. But I cannot believe the same of Antigone and Cordelia – or Tsotsi [a character in a contemporary novel]. I know they are fictions. Does watching them and weeping over them train me into a false mercy, where I take pleasure in my feeling of mercy but perform no merciful action? How can my tears be offered as a sacrifice when I have chosen to consume a tragic story for entertainment? I am haunted by Tsotsi, and I do not know what to do about it.[25]

I admit I am still excited by her using an example from *King Lear*: it is not enough for her to distinguish between secular literature and scripture—the problem of fiction and factuality affects both. But I also admit a bit of envy at her scrupulousness: I think I would have said, "Close enough," either to myself or to one of my children or students, if the example, regardless of its origin, was teaching laudable enough values.

But Carnes is bothered by her example enough, and it is important enough, that she returns to it near the end of her book, with a little more detail to further complicate it: "If Anna and Joachim [the Virgin Mary's parents, named as such in a non-canonical text] may not be historical persons, then how is their reality different from that of Antigone, Merida, or Hermione Granger? What am I doing when I contemplate the image of holy people who may have no historical existence? I do not contemplate *nothing*."[26] She decides then that since thousands of people over the centuries—real, historical people—contemplated these characters, that gives the (possibly) fictional characters some basis in historical reality; even if the original

---

[25]Carnes, *Motherhood*, 54.
[26]Ibid., 157.

characters were fiction, the piety and devotion based on them were real, and now, a contemporary believer can legitimately join in that longstanding and growing community of the faithful in contemplating such characters.

And at that point, I think I can say, "Close enough" to how I'm thinking of the texts examined in this volume and their appropriation, and do so without too many misgivings. And not because it can be noted that *King Lear* was based on earlier texts that have some claim to being based on historical reminiscences (while I also again set aside the question of how much of *Confessions* may be manufactured or embellished); and without inquiring pedantically how many generations of believers would be needed to lend enough historical reality to an originally fictional character. And I would not want the label "holy" for Cordelia or Lear (though I might allow it for Augustine or Monica, though I would not insist on it at all)—"virtuous" would be enough for the kind of secular devotion I had in mind throughout my analysis. I'm more interested in the process Carnes here describes. Joining into a community of interpretation is quite close to how I would imagine anyone who loves these texts and wants to share their truth with others would envision the process of study and interpretation and appropriation, and it is exactly what I would be most pleased and proud of if my analysis invited and helped people to join.

EPILOGUE

As I finish the analytical part of the current volume, I feel some final, partly autobiographical reflections would not be amiss, as I consider again, "Why *Lear*? Why *Confessions*?" The connection to *Confessions* as also partly autobiographical should, I hope, increase how appropriate this move now seems, though I hope the connections to *King Lear* are equally fitting, even if they are less obvious and directly applicable. And I confess (with some more envy) that I have nothing as clearly relevant as the anecdotes Jonathan Bate offers in his similar reflections on Shakespeare and his own life.[1] Though I did have to go through my father's library when he died,[2] he did not have a favorite edition of Shakespeare, as Bate recounts when writing of his father. My father probably would have derided Shakespeare as unrealistic and liking him as pretentious. If he made room for any of his plays, it would probably have been *Macbeth*, with a hero too passionate, impetuous, and ambitious—wavering Hamlet or self-pitying Lear would have only invited scorn and contempt from my father, I suspect. And his library certainly did not contain anything by Augustine (or anything overtly Christian or theological).

But perhaps the bare fact that he had a non-technical library is enough of a hook on which to hang these reflections, or a good enough place to begin them. If you asked me what my father valued or believed in, I would struggle with the question, even today, having had many years to dwell on it. I think typical of some men, especially of an earlier generation, he was not one to even entertain such abstractions. Ask such a man what he likes or prefers, or what he finds hateful, and you'd be more likely to get a concrete and verifiable answer. But values and beliefs were either mysterious or self-evident: either way they were not a topic for discussions, when I was growing up. But other men had concrete things they clung to, and which might give clues of the intellectual or spiritual essence that would have left such a trail of artifacts. And there wasn't much of that in the tiny apartment he was living in when he died. Indeed, the actual apartment looked barely

---

[1] Jonathan Bate, *Mad About Shakespeare: Life Lessons from the Bard* (London: William Collins, 2022).
[2] George G. Paffenroth (1932–2004).

lived-in: he seemed to have been living mostly in his car for some time. The apartment might as well have been a storage locker—everything packed in boxes, undisturbed for months or years. And by "everything," I mean books. Not much else. No family photos, no knick-knacks, no trophies. So I continued my investigation, basing it mostly on the books he had gone to some lengths to keep.

I remember books in every room when I was growing up—spilling off homemade shelves of boards on cinder blocks, when I was very young; packed tightly on store-bought bookcases when I was older. The collection had dwindled over the years—"whittled away" my father might have said—after several cross-country moves and a divorce (a brief, second marriage, not my mother, who had died many years before). But he had still kept a few dozen boxes packed with books—almost all of them modern fiction and history. So his insistence, as I described in my earlier volume (really a mild obsession, one of his friends told me recently), that I go to St. John's College, Annapolis, made some sense (obsession with books), but on the other hand, it was also sort of nonsensical or confused (modern fiction and history are two genres we read almost none of at St. John's). But perhaps I'm trying to be too abstract again, and thinking of what the books are *about*, when he was simply thinking their physical presence was enough, it demonstrated some solidity or permanence, regardless of the content (and in contradistinction to the ephemerality of television or the internet). When I force myself to think that way—of books as objects, not the contents of books—then I think it comes a little more into focus: they were the embodiment for him, of non-instrumental knowledge (to get technical about it), knowledge for its own sake. He was an electrical engineer and fairly skilled at carpentry too, so all of his professional life was spent creating physical objects. But there were no manuals or how-to books—definitely not when I was growing up; we did find one 1950s college textbook, looking somewhat out of place, packed away with all the other books, when cleaning out his apartment. Practical knowledge you learned by doing, not reading—with the corollary that what could be learned by reading was somehow different, separate, mysterious, arcane—sacred if he had made room for that category (and I suppose implicitly he did, as distasteful as he would have found the things usually referred to with that label). The books I was surrounded by when I was a child were all proclamations or advertisements that, "Reading is for pleasure, for entertainment, for beauty – not for practical knowledge or anything as vulgar and venal as how to make money." I see now they were almost secular relics in their own way, sacred and not profane or ordinary. Why else

Epilogue

lug them around, traversing the continent thrice, over forty years? And as I testified to in my earlier volume, that was the idea of St. John's with which he was obsessed—a place where everyone learned for the sake of learning, not because it was practical or profitable. As critical as I may be of him in this Epilogue (and elsewhere), that idea of knowledge for its own sake, an idea that seems to only become rarer as the internet expands and cheapens and degrades all knowledge, or renders it impossible to know anything—that is something worth honoring and thanking him for, and I should emphasize it here at the end. It is a value I have tried (with very mixed results) to carry on and promote in my own life and work, though many will find it as surprising as I have, that such is not always the operative or guiding value in higher education today; but that is probably a subject for another book.

But as I say—no theological volumes there, no favorite edition of Shakespeare (we just had the cheap-o *Complete Works* in a single volume, probably from Waldenbooks in the mall), no Augustine. So my choice of college again comes through pretty directly and literally: if you're raised in a home of someone who is thus obsessed with books, who fills most every horizontal surface with books and then builds or buys more shelving to make more room, then you probably should go to the Great Books school and hang out with others who have been so raised. But if we're looking for thematic influences on my later writing, this whole Epilogue would make more sense for my writing on horror, where youthful reading eventually grew into mature analysis. And to be fuller and more accurate in this description: I did give remarks similar to this Epilogue in my acceptance speech for the Stoker Award in 2007, reminiscing how a house full of books is a house full of ideas to be explored, worlds to discover, problems or questions to explain. As I tease young people now: "back in the day" we only had two dystopian novels—two!—and you all get a new one every month! But I do remember pulling *1984* and *Brave New World* off the shelves at home and reading them at a fairly young age, and looking back now on my writing from about twenty years ago and my reading from fifty years ago, I can see where they stuck with me and mutated under the influence of the movies I'd also grown up watching.

However, I think that is probably trying to trace the influence in the opposite direction than what I am attempting here—trying to look in the past to find themes that will appear later, when now I am looking at a finished product (the current volume) and trying to think of what it summons up from my past, where these literary works connect to my memories of my real, lived experience. And I think the first place I go in my memory, after

Augustine's Confessions and Shakespeare's King Lear

I've written a book on variously traumatic or salvific or revelatory family relationships, is to the days spent sorting through my father's belongings after he died. As I've said, the first thing that struck me (then or now) was the dearth of items overall, and the preponderance of books. (And all of us who've had to pack and move books, as much as we love them, at some point in the process, we curse their weight and density, and wish we had been a little more circumspect in collecting them, or had chosen to collect bottle caps or postage stamps.) But as I think more about the scene, I have to bring in the other characters involved in the apartment cleaning. I was helped with the whole task by a childhood friend, Bill. Obviously, I didn't pick him deliberately or specifically for this task: it was serendipity that he just happened to live in Los Angeles, which is coincidentally where my father had moved years before because southern California is a big center for both the entertainment industry (in which Bill works) and the aerospace industry (in which my father had worked). But it strikes me now as completely appropriate—like if I had been asked, years before, who should help me sort through my father's belongings years in the future, who would be best at and most helpful at the task, I probably would have chosen Bill. My father was not someone who was easy to get to know, garrulous or outgoing, but Bill had some memories of interactions (funny or serious or odd—but most importantly, none of them sentimental) with him over the years, and such made our work in my father's apartment much easier (for me). There are painful, difficult tasks and times, for which the only right companion and helper (or at least, the best one, if he's available) is a longtime friend, and not a romantic partner or a family member, who would complicate the whole ordeal and make it more difficult. I'm not sure I knew that before that week in LA, but I've known it since—and now, the middle scenes of *King Lear*, with the Fool and Kent, Gloucester and Edgar, sticking by Lear when they don't "have to" (but who must definitely act like they "have to"), make much more sense to me, and ring more true, as a depiction of male bonding and healing.[3] And equally true and perhaps more importantly: that week in LA (which at the time mostly just seemed confusing and exhausting), now makes more sense to me, whenever I see a production of *King Lear*.

---

[3]Though I shouldn't over emphasize the "male" part of the bonding: one of the few elements of the recent Branagh production of *King Lear* that worked well for me, was the casting of Kent as a woman (played by Eleanor de Rohan), though in her disguise as Caius she presents as male. But it impressed on me that the crucial point in the storm is that Lear be surrounded by longtime friends and not family members or romantic partners.

Epilogue

To return to the topic of my father's books and to fine tune one comment I made earlier: he had no theological books in his collection when I was growing up, but when he died, he'd acquired a couple from my sending him copies of the books I'd written. And he hadn't packed these away. I don't think they were displayed, per se, but they were not sealed up in a box. One of the days Bill and I went to the apartment to clean it out, we invited one of the women my father had been dating to come along. (I say "one of" because when I listened to his answering machine, it was clear several different women had been trying unsuccessfully to contact my father in the days since he had collapsed on his apartment floor. So I had to make those awkward, death notification contacts to women I'd never met. But one woman seemed to be more of a commitment than the others, and I therefore felt deserved more information and inclusion in our work.) I gifted her the small stack of my books and told her to take whatever else she wanted. (There was nothing in there from my childhood, except books, nothing of sentimental value; I think she took a lamp.) She said she remembered when my father had gotten one of my books in the mail; she said she had told him to tell me he was proud of me, and wondered if he had. He had, though in an extremely awkward way. "I. Am ... Proud ... Of you"—Bill Shatner could not have made the pauses and emphases more unnatural and halting. And really, to be completely accurate, it was not only unexpected, coming from him, but a unique experience in the course of my life. All of it had been so unusual that I probably had already suspected a woman had suggested the gesture to him, and now that was confirmed.

Which takes us to the most obvious parallel, much more so than the faithful dedication of the Fool and Kent and Bill—Lear's emotional fragility, as rigid and inflexible and easily shattered into sharp and dangerous shards as glass—I don't think I was ever unaware that the opening scene of *King Lear* reads exactly like a frequent and familiar explosion in my home growing up, and since. To be precise, and fairer: not as to the demand for an affirmation—my father was not so overt and demanding and would have considered any show of affection in either direction as vulgar and demeaning. And Lear's anger is absurdly volcanic, while my father's was more seething, sulking, simmering, brooding. But the fragility, and taking any deviation from his point of view or his plans as an unforgivable assault on his authority or even his identity: my father displayed those parts of Lear's horrible personality on a weekly basis. And if it didn't make me and my mother as fawning and eagerly accommodating as Goneril and Regan, nor did it make us as courageous and boldly frank as Cordelia and Kent: Cordelia's asides in the opening scene seem much more realistic and believable to me, as the most likely and frequent coping mechanisms (cowering, avoidance, furtive whispers, and silence) for living with such a toxic and volatile combination of male authority that lacks any ability to dialogue, discuss, or compromise, but which only reacts by being hurt and enraged at any challenge (and which treats any disagreement as a challenge), and lashes out with curses and insults.

But in sifting through my father's meager possessions and the memories they summoned of my childhood, I think it was his lack of connection to any place or thing that next struck me and occupied my thoughts. I remember the anxiety and tears, growing up, at having to move every couple of years. And as his overflowing answering machine attested: his connections to people were numerous (more numerous than mine, if I'm being honest), but rather tenuous, once my mother was dead and I was grown and moved out of the house. When someone asks now where I grew up and I rattle off the list, they always ask, "Oh, was your father in the military?" as that is the only lifestyle where such constant mobility would make sense to most people. But no, though he had been in the Army during the Korean War, afterward and throughout my childhood, he just changed jobs frequently, by choice. (And to be fair, quite successfully, always moving up in salary and position.) So Augustine's upward mobility, several times moving across North Africa and Italy, strikes me as normal in a way that would cause many people to remark on the unusualness of such transience. Though I can remind myself that most people in antiquity lived their entire lives within walking distance of where they had been born, I don't need that reminder to understand and identify with Augustine's less typical lifestyle—it seems perfectly ordinary and unremarkable to me, given my experience. But on that point, it is not Augustine with whom I identify, but with his mother and the concubine, following him around to places not of their own choosing, since that is how I experienced such a life, growing up. It makes me marvel anew at Monica's faith and serenity, when she is able to let go of any preference for where she dies or is buried, when I know throughout my life I've longed to stay put, to have a home from which I would not be uprooted and catapulted thousands of miles away, with little warning and complete assurance it would happen again in a couple of years. Which then makes me wonder: are some people forced into transience and they abandon the lifestyle as soon as they are able, while others are "real" wanderers, really can't stay put or put down roots? Augustine, as we saw, eventually gave up on the upward mobility, and he wound up relatively close to his starting point in North Africa; I am

Epilogue

sitting right now, in a home I moved into more than twenty-three years ago, and it is located 80 miles from where I was born—maybe not quite walking distance, but just an hour and a half drive. The default for Augustine and myself apparently was to settle down eventually, regardless of what came before, whereas my father moved across the width of North America three times (plus a stint in the army that took him across North America and the Pacific, all the way to Korea), and finally ended up 3,000 miles from where he'd begun (and even now, I feel like he would've gone farther if he could have, the way Dante imagines Odysseus not staying in Ithaca after all his travails but setting sail again, because that's just who he was, just what he wanted, the only life he could imagine, the only one that would satisfy him).

It scares me, even, to think maybe I have inherited or am falling into such urges, or developing such habits myself. I find myself tossing a change of clothes into the back of my car, in case I need it later that day, and I feel a sudden, passing anxiety that maybe something terrible is taking hold of me and I'm just a couple of steps away from living in my car as my father had ended up doing. But before I get too worked up, I think more generally about the relative importance of place, of feeling connected or rooted, and how it might vary naturally in different people, or change over the course of their lives. It has been a consistently successful paper prompt, when I teach *King Lear*, to ask how Lear's location in castles or on the heath, changes his outlook or behavior, and contemplating moving between different locations gradually loses some of its terror and the recollections of trauma fade for me, and becomes more of a challenge or even an opportunity. It also makes me think of how different and yet recognizably similar people are from their parents and therefore the threat of some genetic determinism is not as scary as it might seem at first. In my writing and analysis in this volume, this has come out as considering the family resemblance and radical differences between Augustine and his parents, or between Lear and his daughters; or in my personal life, even on this specific point of connection to place, by considering the evolving lives of my children, and how I recognize but am surprised anew at seeing different elements of myself now expressed in such different and evolving people. My son is already married and owns a home and really seems to crave that rootedness and stability, while my daughter is still moving around constantly, both with travel and with changing jobs and relocating, almost uncannily like my father, whom she never knew.

For a bigger sweep of time and distance, I am reminded of how during the pandemic I took my daughter to show her where some of our ancestors were buried at the beginning of the twentieth century, as it was information that would otherwise die with me, if I didn't show it to someone. In retrospect, the whole scene was bizarre, almost comical: on a day when we were on lockdown, forbidden contact with other living people, I was driving my daughter a fair distance to see crudely carved headstones of people we'd never met, people with whom we had very little in common besides our last name. Further increasing the strangeness factor, the graveyard was incongruously located now adjacent to an elementary school's playground, though both were eerily vacant and silent on this plague-ridden day. But on the way there, I saw vividly how differently my daughter related to the physical surroundings than I ever had. The drive takes one through a change in topography rather suddenly and remarkably. Moving down from hills and groves, a huge plain of inky black dirt was spread before us, with a single two lane road crossing the dirt plain until it reached a hill of trees rising up out of the black expanse—the aptly named Pine Island, which is where our group of Paffenroths came from Ellis Island, 60 miles to the southeast, in several batches starting about 120 years previously. My daughter asked me to pull over to examine the ground more closely. Kneeling, she was quite excited, cupping both her hands to hold up a scoop of dirt. Besides its almost unnaturally black color, it also felt unexpectedly fine, silky, not gritty or cold or damp. But though I could remark on its unusual qualities, I did not feel the excitement my daughter seemed to as she held the soil. I had heard that this soil was "good" (though as an urbanite or suburbanite I still have no idea what that means, really), and its reputation as such had attracted our ancestors and many others, but I had never seen firsthand, someone getting as excited, almost ecstatic at some dirt and its "goodness" in such a physical, visceral, tactile way, as my literate, erudite daughter was that morning. I have lived all over North America and traveled all over Europe and North America, and I have never before thought of or even noticed the quality of the dirt I had been standing on. But seeing her handling and touching this dirt, letting it run through her fingers and even breathing in its scent, made it seem much more understandable, even inevitable, that people quite similar to us, just a couple of generations before us, would have felt so irresistibly drawn to it that they journeyed 5,000 miles for this dirt (as their ancestors had uprooted themselves to move almost 2,000 miles a couple of generations before that, based on the reputed quality of other dirt). All I could think was, "I guess she got the dirt-loving gene after it skipped a couple of generations."

And lest this seem like a Trumpian rant about sharks and electrocution and windmills, let me try to summarize what I am exploring and claiming here with these examples, before I draw a conclusion: to note parallels or analogies between real life and events described in literature, as I'm trying to do in this Epilogue, is to multiply the total number of examples we can use in comparisons, as we try to make sense of the events we're examining—which is to say, of the lives we are living. To say, "That reminds me of the time when I …" and "That reminds me of this scene in a book I read, or in a play or movie I saw" are both relevant and become increasingly helpful and potentially revealing, as we work to articulate how and why they compare.

And although I began these autobiographical reflections with my father, and have come back to him on several points, the texts I've analyzed both get their centeredness, if you will, from an absent mother—Augustine in reflecting upon the death of his mother, the mother from whom he fled, even as he found himself—in spite of himself—following her example; *King Lear* with the dysfunction of three grown daughters and their father, with a mother so absent we readers have no idea when or how she died, or even her name, the characters' silence on her existence is so absolute and impenetrable. And likewise, my mother's death when I was fourteen,[4] her absence for most of my life, has shaped who I am and the kinds of books I find most interesting, and how I analyze them, much more than my father, who died much later (when I was 38). While perhaps he was always absent in important emotional or spiritual ways, he was physically present for much more of my life; she was physically absent, however much I have wanted or thought (felt?) of her presence. Of course, I don't know all my father's attitudes or beliefs, but I have much more to go on with him than I do in speculating what my mother's might have been. I feel like I knew him more fully, and can give some account of how I ended up the way I am, under his influence, whereas my mother has been an unknown and a mystery, for the vast majority of my life. So really, the answer to, "Why do I study and write about these two books?" turns out to be embarrassingly simple and straightforward, in one sense: because my mother died when I was quite young, and these books identify with and center themselves on a similar or related experience of an absent mother.

A further but perhaps more difficult and even troubling question to ask, however, would be, "What does studying these texts do for me now?" and I return to the title of the Introduction, "Origins and Ends": I have now found the plausible origins of these ideas, but what are their ends? To trace their study to some fact of my autobiography answers one sense of "Why?"

---

[4]Gloria May Paffenroth (1930–1980).

but leaves another sense of, "So what?" rather frustratingly unanswered. The most interesting question is not, "What is the origin or background of this study? Where did it come from?" But rather, "What is the purpose or outcome of this study? Why keep studying it, going forward?" That is what I have been trying, in real time, to trace in this Epilogue, to work out in my own mind what I think of what I've been doing, now that I've done it. I think it is to see how works of literature, texts that have been deliberately created with artifice, choices, calculation (even if *Confessions* is based on real events, and *King Lear* more distantly influenced by historical reminiscences), resemble our real, lived reality—broadly, or on specific points. And by that resemblance, to consider that reality, too, might be as beautiful and meaningful as the literature we study. That is what had for so long been confounding and causing me pain because when reality happened to me—well, it just happened. "It is what it is," as the kids say, about literally everything, but apathy or non-judgment is not what is needed, I see now. My mother's death, or my own debilitating (and now chronic) illness three years ago, was just a cataclysm, an unforeseen disaster, when it actually occurred. All that could be reasonably done about it now would be to accept it as stoically as possible. But if, on the other hand, the scrutiny and aesthetic and moral judgments we bring to a work of literature like *King Lear* or *Confessions*, which tell us how to understand its beauty and meaning—if those tools of analysis also work on real life, even if just analogously or roughly, then they should also be applied to it, and yield at least heuristic interpretations, suggestions, perspectives from which we can see our experience as well as these works of literature, as beautiful and meaningful, and not just "as is," as events to be appreciated or even cherished, not just endured.

BIBLIOGRAPHY

Achilleos, Stella. "Sovereignty, Social Contract, and the State of Nature in *King Lear*." In *The Routledge Companion to Shakespeare and Philosophy*. Craig Bourne and Emily Caddick Bourne, editors. London and New York: Routledge, 2019. Pp. 267–78.

Armstrong, Liz. "*King Lear* Banned in England?" Online at https://www.bard.org/news/king-lear-banned-in-england/ (accessed November 7, 2024).

Asiedu, Felix B. A. "Following the Example of a Woman: Augustine's Conversion to Christianity in 386." *Vigiliae Christianae* 57.3 (August 2003) 276–306.

Atkinson, Clarissa W. "'Your Servant, My Mother': The Figure of Saint Monica in the Ideology of Christian Motherhood." In Clarissa W. Atkinson, Constance H. Buchanan, and Margaret R. Miles, editors. *Immaculate & Powerful: The Female in Sacred Image and Social Reality*. The Harvard Women's Studies in Religion series. Boston: Beacon Press, 1985. Pp. 139–72.

Baker, Naomi. "'This Sad Time': The Augustinian Temporality of *King Lear*." *Modern Philology* 120.3 (2023) 335–55.

Bamber, Linda. *Comic Women, Tragic Men: A Study of Gender and Genre in Shakespeare*. Stanford, CA: Stanford University Press, 1982.

Bate, Jonathan. *Mad About Shakespeare: Life Lessons from the Bard*. London: William Collins, 2022.

Bidgoli, Mehrdad. "Ethics, Subjectivity, and Alterity in *King Lear*: On Cordelia's Defiance and Sacrifice." *Religion and the Arts: A Journal from Boston College* 25.4 (2021) 385–420.

Bloom, Harold. *Shakespeare: The Invention of the Human*. New York: Riverhead Books, 1998.

Boulding, Maria, translator. *The Confessions*. Editor John E. Rotelle. Hyde Park, NY: New City Press, 1997.

Bouwman, Kitty. "Spiritual Motherhood of Monica: Two Mothers in the Life of Saint Augustine." *Studies in Spirituality* 29 (2019) 49–69.

Bowery, Anne-Marie. "Monica: The Feminine Face of Christ." In *Feminist Interpretations of Augustine*. Judith Chelius Stark, editor. University Park, PA: Pennsylvania State University Press, 2007. Pp. 69–95.

Brown, Peter. *Augustine of Hippo: A Biography*. Forty-Fifth Anniversary Edition. Berkeley and Los Angeles: University of California Press, 2000. (First published 1967.)

Burrus, Virginia, and Catherine Keller. "Confessing Monica." In *Feminist Interpretations of Augustine*. Judith Chelius Stark, editor. University Park, PA: Pennsylvania State University Press, 2007. Pp. 119–45.

Bibliography

Burzynska, Katarzyna. "'Nothing Will Come out of Nothing': The Existential Dimension of Interpersonal Relationships in *King Lear*." In *The Routledge Companion to Shakespeare and Philosophy*. Craig Bourne and Emily Caddick Bourne, editors. London and New York: Routledge, 2019. Pp. 363-73.

Bush, Geoffrey. *Shakespeare and the Natural Condition*. Cambridge, MA: Harvard University Press, 1956.

Carnes, Natalie. *Motherhood: A Confession*. Stanford, CA: Stanford University Press, 2020.

Cavell, Stanley. *Disowning Knowledge: In Six Plays of Shakespeare*. Cambridge: Cambridge University Press, 1987.

Chadwick, Henry. *Augustine: A Very Short Introduction*. Oxford: Oxford University Press, 1986.

Clark, Gillian. *Monica: An Ordinary Saint*. Oxford, New York: Oxford University Press, 2015.

Conybeare, Catherine. *The Irrational Augustine*. Oxford: Oxford University Press, 2006.

Cooper, Kate. *Queens of a Fallen World: The Lost Women of Augustine's Confessions*. London: Basic Books, 2023.

Coyle, J. Kevin. "In Praise of Monica: A Note on the Ostia Experience of *Confessions* IX." *Augustinian Studies* 13 (1982) 87-96.

Curran, Kevin, editor. *Shakespeare and Judgment*. Edinburgh: Edinburgh University Press, 2017.

Da Silva, Francisco Vaz. "Sexual Horns: The Anatomy and Metaphysics of Cuckoldry in European Folklore." *Comparative Studies in Society and History* 48.2 (April 2006) 396-418.

Davies, Oliver Ford. *Shakespeare's Fathers and Daughters*. Bloomsbury Arden Shakespeare. London: Bloomsbury, 2017.

Davis, Matthew M. "'My Master Calls Me': Authority and Loyalty in *King Lear*." *Renascence* 70.1 (Wint 2018) 59-78.

Djuth, Marianne. "Augustine, Monica, and the Love of Wisdom." *Augustinian Studies* 39.2 (2008) 217-32.

Dumm, Thomas. *Loneliness as a Way of Life*. Cambridge, MA: Harvard University Press, 2008.

Dunnington, Kent. "Humility: An Augustinian Perspective." *Pro Ecclesia: A Journal of Catholic and Evangelical Theology* 25.1 (Winter 2016) 18-43.

Eagleton, Terry. *Trouble with Strangers: A Study of Ethics*. West Sussex, UK: Wiley-Blackwell, 2009.

Finn, Douglas. "The Holy Spirit and the Church in the Earliest Augustine: An Analysis of the Character of Monnica in the Cassiciacum Dialogues." *Papers Presented at the Seventeenth International Conference on Patristic Studies* 24 (2017) 141-65.

Foakes, Reginald Anthony. *Hamlet Versus Lear: Cultural Politics and Shakespeare's Art*. Cambridge: Cambridge University Press, 1993.

Foulcher, Jane. *Reclaiming Humility: Four Studies in the Monastic Tradition*. Collegeville, MN: Liturgical Press, 2015.

Gil, Daniel Juan. *Shakespeare's Anti-Politics: Sovereign Power and the Life of the Flesh*. London: Palgrave Macmillan, 2013.

Gladwin, Michael. "Embodying Humility in Augustine's *Confessions*." *St. Mark's Review* 256.2 (June/July 2021) 53–65.

Goethe, Johann Wolfgang von. *Goethe's Faust*. Trans. by Walter Kaufmann. New York: Anchor Books, 1962.

Graham, Kenneth J. E. "'Without the Form of Justice': Plainness and the Performance of Love in *King Lear*." *Shakespeare Quarterly* 42.4 (Winter 1991) 438–61.

Greenberg, Mitchell. "The Concept of 'Early Modern'." *Journal for Early Modern Cultural Studies* 13.2 (Spring 2013) 75–9.

Greenblatt, Stephen. *Shakespeare's Freedom*. Chigago and London: University of Chicago Press, 2010.

Greenfield, Thelma Nelson. "The Clothing Motif in *King Lear*." *Shakespeare Quarterly* 5.3 (1954) 281–6.

Hagberg, Garry L. "Lear as a Tragedy of Errors: 'He hath ever but slenderly known himself'." In *The Routledge Companion to Shakespeare and Philosophy*. Craig Bourne and Emily Caddick Bourne, editors. London and New York: Routledge, 2019. Pp. 121–32.

Hamlin, Hannibal. "Review of Kim Paffenroth: *On King Lear, The Confessions, and Human Experience and Nature*." *Augustinian Studies* 54.1 (2023) 117–21.

Harper, Elizabeth. "'A Disease That's in My Flesh Which I Must Needs Call Mine': Lear, Macbeth and the Fear of Futurity." *English Studies* 100.6 (2019) 604–26.

Haste, Matthew. "'So Many Voices': The Piety of Monica, Mother of Augustine." *The Journal of Family Ministry* 4 (2013) 6–10.

Higginbotham, Jennifer. *The Girlhood of Shakespeare's Sisters: Gender, Transgression, Adolescence*. Edinburgh Critical Studies in Renaissance Culture. Edinburgh: Edinburgh University Press, 2013.

Holte, Ragnar. "Monica, 'the Philosopher.'" *Augustinus* 39 (1994) 293–316.

Kahan, Jeffrey. "Introduction." In *King Lear: New Critical Essays*. Jeffrey Kahan, editor. Shakespeare Criticism, vol. 33. New York and London: Routledge, 2008. Pp. 1–103.

Kahn, Coppélia. *Man's Estate: Masculine Identity in Shakespeare*. Berkeley: University of California Press, 1981.

Kalpakgian, Mitchell. "*King Lear*: The Attack on Fatherhood and the Destruction of Hierarchy." *Catholic Social Science Review* 3 (1998) 163–72.

Kearney, James. "'This Is Above All Strangeness': *King Lear*, Ethics, and the Phenomenology of Recognition." *Criticism* 54.3 (2012) 455–67.

Kelly, Philippa. "See What Breeds about Her Heart: *King Lear*, Feminism, and Performance." *Renaissance Drama* 33 (2004) 137–57.

Kottman, Paul A. *Tragic Conditions in Shakespeare: Disinheriting the Globe*. Baltimore: Johns Hopkins University Press, 2009.

Lawrence, Sean K. "'Gods That We Adore': The Divine in *King Lear*." *Renascence* 56.3 (2004) 143–59.

Bibliography

Levenson, Carl Avren. "Distance and Presence in Augustine's 'Confessions.'" *The Journal of Religion* 65.4 (October 1985) 500–12.

McDuffie, Felecia. "Augustine's Rhetoric of the Feminine in the *Confessions*: Woman as Mother, Woman as Other." In *Feminist Interpretations of Augustine*. Judith Chelius Stark, editor. University Park, PA: Pennsylvania State University Press, 2007. Pp. 97–118.

McInerney, Joseph J. Foreword by C. C. Pecknold. *The Greatness of Humility: St. Augustine on Moral Excellence*. Cambridge, England: James Clarke, 2017.

Miles, Margaret R. "Infancy, Parenting, and Nourishment in Augustine's '*Confessions*.'" *Journal of the American Academy of Religion* 50.3 (September 1982) 349–64.

Miles, Margaret R. "Not Nameless but Unnamed: The Woman Torn from Augustine's Side." In *Feminist Interpretations of Augustine*. Judith Chelius Stark, editor. University Park, PA: Pennsylvania State University Press, 2007. Pp. 167–188.

Moore, Rebecca. "O Mother, Where Art Thou? In Search of Saint Monnica." In *Feminist Interpretations of Augustine*. Judith Chelius Stark, editor. University Park, PA: Pennsylvania State University Press, 2007. Pp. 147–66.

Nock, Arthur Darby. *Conversion: The Old and the New in Religion from Alexander the Great to Augustine of Hippo*. Oxford: Oxford University Press, 1933.

North, Anna. "President Trump's King Lear Moment." *New York Times*, May 17, 2017. Online at https://www.nytimes.com/2017/05/17/opinion/president-trumps-king-lear-moment.html (accessed May 19, 2025).

Norton, Tom. "Donald Trump Syphilis Rumors: Doctors Weigh In." *Newsweek*, January 19, 2024. Online at https://www.newsweek.com/donald-trump-syphilis-rumors-doctors-weigh-1861983 (accessed May 19, 2025).

Novy, Marianne. *Love's Argument: Gender Relations in Shakespeare*. Chapel Hill and London: University of North Carolina Press, 1984.

Oh, Elisa. "Refusing to Speak: Silent, Chaste, and Disobedient Female Subjects in *King Lear* and The Tragedy of Mariam." *Explorations in Renaissance Culture* 34.2 (Winter 2008) 185–216.

Paffenroth, Kim. *On King Lear, the Confessions, and Human Experience and Nature*. Reading Augustine Series. New York: Bloomsbury Publishing, 2021.

Pardue, Stephen. "Kenosis and Its Discontents: Towards an Augustinian Account of Divine Humility." *Scottish Journal of Theology* 65.3 (2012) 271–88.

Park, Eonjoo. "Sympathy for Old Age in *King Lear*." *ANQ: A Quarterly Journal of Short Articles, Notes and Reviews* 34.3 (2021) 193–8.

Ruddy, Deborah Wallace. "The Humble God: Healer, Mediator, and Sacrifice." *Logos: A Journal of Catholic Thought and Culture* 7.3 (2004) 87–108.

Ryan, Kiernan. "Shakespeare's Inhumanity." *Shakespeare Survey* 66 (2013) 220–31.

Sanderson, David. "Why Shakespeare Had Woman Trouble." *The Times*, October 10, 2018, p. 23. https://www.thetimes.com/article/shakespeare-s-misogyny-may-be-explained-by-his-syphilis-7xsh8mc0j (accessed May 19, 2025).

Schlabach, Gerald W. "Augustine's Hermeneutic of Humility: An Alternative to Moral Imperialism and Moral Relativism." *The Journal of Religious Ethics* 22.2 (1994) 299–330.

Schulman, Alex. *Rethinking Shakespeare's Political Philosophy: From Lear to Leviathan*. Edinburgh: Edinburgh University Press, 2014.

Sehorn, John. "Monica as Synecdoche for the Pilgrim Church in the *Confessiones*." 46.2 (2015) 225–48.

Selleck, Nancy. "Interpersonal Soliloquy: Self and Audience in Shakespeare and Augustine." *English Literary Renaissance* 51.1 (2021) 63–95.

Sheerin, Brian. "Making Use of Nothing: The Sovereignties of *King Lear*." *Studies in Philology* 110.4 (2013) 789–811.

Smith, Richard Upsher, "Saint Monica and Lady Philosophy." *Carmina Philosophiae* 18 (2009) 93–125.

Soloski, Alexis. "King Lear review – Glenda Jackson Dominates Flawed Broadway Show." *The Guardian*, April 4, 2019. https://www.theguardian.com/stage/2019/apr/04/king-lear-shakespeare-glenda-jackson-broadway (accessed November 7, 2024).

Sundelson, David. *Shakespeare's Restoration of the Father*. New Brunswick, NJ: Rutgers University Press, 1983.

Tambling, Jeremy. "Comfort and Despair in *King Lear*." *Essays in Criticism* 70.1 (January 2020) 38–63.

Tishman, Esther Lisa Freinkel. "Review of Kim Paffenroth: *On King Lear, the Confessions, and Human Experience and Nature*." *Augustiniana* 72.3–4 (2022) 427–30.

Van Oort, Johannes. "Monnica's Bishop and the 'filius istarum lacrimarum' (*Conf.* 3,21)." *Church History and Religious Culture* 103 (2023) 1–21.

Ward, Graham. "Extremities." *Modern Theology* 34.2 (April 2018) 235–42.

Wasserman, Jerry. "'And Every One Have Need of Other': Bond and Relationship in *King Lear*." *Mosaic: An Interdisciplinary Critical Journal* 9.2 (Winter 1976) 15–30.

Wetzel, James. "The Trappings of Woe and Confessions of Grief." In *A Reader's Companion to Augustine's Confessions*. Kim Paffenroth and Robert Kennedy, editors. Louisville and London: Westminster John Knox, 2003. Pp. 53–69.

Winchester, Daniel. "Converting to Continuity: Temporality and Self in Eastern Orthodox Conversion Narratives." *Journal for the Scientific Study of Religion* 54.3 (2015) 439–60.

Wright, David. "Monnica's Baptism, Augustine's Deferred Baptism, and Patricius." *Augustinian Studies* 29.2 (1998) 1–17.

Young, Bruce W. "*King Lear* and the Calamity of Fatherhood." In *In the Company of Shakespeare: Essays on English Renaissance Literature in Honor of G. Blakemore Evans*. Thomas Moisan and Douglas Bruster, editors. Madison and Teaneck, NJ: Fairleigh Dickinson University Press, 2002. Pp. 43–64.

INDEX

Achilleos, Stella 29, 31, 32, 36, 40
Acts, Book of 1
Adeodatus 64
Albany 39, 79, 80
Alypius 26
Ambrose 26
Aristotle 12, 25
Armstrong, Liz 76
Asiedu, Felix B. A. 63, 64, 65
Atkinson, Clarissa W. 58, 69, 72
Augustine 2–4, 7–27, 29, 45, 47, 52, 53, 55–73, 91–2, 94–8, 101–2, 105, 107, 110, 111, 112

babies *see* sin
Baker, Naomi 98
Bate, Jonathan 105
Beatrice 56
Bennett, Madeleine vii
Bidgoli, Mehrdad 33, 85
Bloom, Harold 34, 36, 39, 42, 43, 46, 53, 77, 82, 87, 95
Boethius 57
Bouwman, Kitty 56, 68, 73
Bowery, Anne-Marie 72
Branagh, Kenneth 42, 94, 108
Brave New World 107
Brown, Peter 8, 9
Burrus, Virginia 72, 73
Bush, Geoffrey 92, 99, 100

Campbell University vi
Carnes, Natalie 59, 63, 73, 85, 102, 103
Cassiciacum 26, 68–70
Christ 23–4, 52
Cicero 19
Clark, Gillian 55, 58, 59
Cleary, Scott vi
Commedia 56
concubine 57, 64, 65, 67, 68, 73, 110

Confessions 1–4, 8–23, 25, 27, 29, 31, 47, 52, 55–73, 75, 76, 91, 94, 97, 99, 101–3, 105, 114
Cooper, Kate 55, 57, 64, 66, 68, 69
Cordelia 30, 32–8, 50, 51, 81, 89, 92–5, 103, 109
Cornwall 39, 51
COVID *see* pandemic
Coyle, J. Kevin 72
cuckoo 80, 84, 88

Dante 56, 111
Da Silva, Francisco Vaz 80
Davis, Matthew M. 37, 38, 39, 40, 51
Dead Poets Society 13
Djiuth, Marianne 57, 58, 68, 69, 70, 72
Dunnington, Kent 23, 24, 25, 26, 47

Edgar 30, 48–50, 108
Edmund 29, 51, 82, 92
Ellis Island 112
evil *see* sin

Faust 92
Finn, Douglas 57, 68, 69
Fool 31, 39, 44, 46, 47, 49, 108, 109
Foulcher, Jane 24, 25
friends/friendship 16–17, 20–1, 26, 27

Gagnon, Alysha vii
Gathje, Michael vi
Gil, Daniel Juan 41, 42, 44, 96
Gladwin, Michael 26, 47
Gloucester 29, 48–50, 87, 108
God 2–4, 13, 14, 16, 18, 25, 26, 29, 47, 48, 51–3, 61–4, 66, 68–70, 91, 94, 97
gods 42, 44, 86, 94
Goethe, Johann Wolfgang von 92
Goneril 29–30, 31–3, 35–40, 43–5, 49–52, 76–8, 80, 81, 83–6, 88, 89, 109
Graham, Kenneth J. E. 32, 34, 37

Index

Greenberg, Mitchell 101
Greenblatt, Stephen 31, 48, 53, 54
Greenfield, Thelma Nelson 41

Hamlet 99–100
Hamlin, Hannibal 2, 3
Hampsey, Casey vi
Harper, Elizabeth 85
Harris, Angela vii
Haste, Matthew 59, 66
Helmrich, Ed vi
Hollingworth, Miles vi
Holte, Ragnar 71
Hortensius 19
humiliation 29–30
humility 23–6, 31, 43–54

infants *see* sin

Jackson, Glenda 76
Justina 57

Kahan, Jeffrey 91
Kalpakgian, Mitchell 85
Keller, Catherine 72, 73
Kelly, Philippa 75
Kennedy, Robert vi
Kent 30, 37–9, 44, 47, 93, 108, 109
King Lear (character) 4, 7, 8, 9, 27, 29–54, 75–90, 91–6, 99, 103, 108, 109, 111
King Lear (play) 1–4, 9, 29–54, 56, 75–90, 91–4, 96–100, 103, 105, 108, 109, 111, 112, 114
Tate version of 91
Korean War 110
Kurosawa, Akira 90

language 12–13
Lawrence, Sean K. 82, 97
Lebeda, Bill viii, 108, 109
Levenson, Carl Avren 61
Lewandowski, Alyssa vii
libido dominandi 12, 21
Los Angeles 108
love 4, 18, 32–6, 52–3
Luke, Gospel of 1

Macbeth 105
Manichees/Manichean 10, 15, 19, 57

Mark, Gospel of 1
McDonald, Wanda vii
McDuffie, Felicia 65
McInerney, Joseph J. 12, 15, 22, 24
Miles, Margaret R. 55, 56, 57, 65, 67, 68
misogyny 75–8, 88–90
Monica/Monnica 26, 27, 55–73, 94, 96, 98, 110, 112
  as mother 57–64
  as philosopher 68–73
  contrasted with Augustine 58–61
  negative/sinful aspects of 60–5
Moore, Rebecca 59
mother/motherhood 57–64, 82

nature 81–2
Nebridius 26
1984 107
Nock, Arthur Darby 45
North, Anna 76
Norton, Tom 76
Notre Dame, University of vi
Novy, Marianne 11, 31, 76, 77, 78, 87, 88, 93, 95, 96

Odysseus 111
Oh, Elisa 81
Ostia 70–2, 92
Oswald 30, 38, 39

Paffenroth, Charles vii, 111
Paffenroth, George G. 105–13
Paffenroth, Gloria May 113
Paffenroth, Sophia vii, 111, 112
Palladino, Richard vi
pandemic (COVID) 2, 3
Park, Eonjoo 77, 85
Perrier, Danny vii
Pine Island 112
Plato/Platonists/Platonism 23, 101–2
Ponticianus 26
power
  in *Confessions* 7–27
  in *King Lear* 29–54
prayer 25–6, 68, 81
Prodigal Son 57

Ran (1985) 90
Regan 29–30, 32, 33, 35–8, 40, 41, 43–5, 48–52, 76–8, 82–6, 88, 89, 109

Index

Rohan, Eleanor de 108
Ruddy, Deborah Wallace 23, 24, 29, 52

Sanderson, David 75
Sawchuk, Natalka C. vi
Schlabach, Gerald W. 15, 24, 25, 26
Schulman, Alex 35, 41, 48, 49, 50, 51, 52, 53
Sehorn, John 57
Selleck, Nancy 96
Shatner, William 109
Sheerin, Brian 29, 31, 39, 52, 53, 94
Simplicianus 26
sin/sinfulness 10–23, 27, 60–5, 101
as possession/possessiveness 22–4
Smith, Richard Upsher 57
Soloski, Alexis 76
St. Francis Xavier University vi
St. John's College vi, 106–7
Stackhouse, Amy vi
Stoker Award 107

syphilis 75–6

Tishman, Esther Lisa Freinkel 2, 3, 53–4
Truffin, Sherry vi
Trump, Donald J. 3, 76, 112

Van Oort, Johannes 57
Varker, Emily vii
Verdi, John vi
Victorinus 26

Wasserman, Jerry 34, 35, 36, 37, 44, 49, 50, 97, 100
Wetzel, James 21
Winchester, Daniel 45
Wisdom 70–2, 94
women
in *Confessions* 27, 55–73, 92
in *King Lear* 43, 52, 75–90, 92
Wray, Charlotte vi